The Spiritual Fruitcake

By

Keith Forrest

DEDICATION

To Caroline, Matt, Steph, Kayleigh, Vince & Lola

For your support – always.

CONTENTS

ACKNOWLEDGMENTS

There are so many people I want to thank - reminds me of the longest Oscar acceptance speech ever – and I am conscious that I may miss someone so my apologies in advance.
Special mention to all my family and friends for their tolerance , support and understanding during this book writing process.

Huge thanks to John Heffernan for helping me with all the technical aspects of my website and book software.

To all those who reviewed my pre-launch edits and offered invaluable insight and advice including Kristi Saar Duarte, Roma Downey, Moyra Irving, David Strang, Dave Green, Rod Wheat, Steve Sturgeon.
All the members of the Acoustic Rainbow band: Matt Forrest, Vish, Nigel Evans & Derek Holt .

INTRODUCTION

Do you want to live a life full of *happiness*, *peace* of mind and enjoy good *health*?
Of course, you do!

I guarantee, *yes guarantee*, that if you follow at least some of the guidelines contained in this book you will at the very least witness major improvements in these three areas;

- happiness,
- peace of mind and
- good health.

You may even find that your life will change beyond belief, and I am talking from first-hand experience as the key points described here most certainly changed mine.

What gives me the right to advise you about how to live your life and how do I know the ideas in this book will work for you?

This book is a Journey, a road trip to the discovery of happiness, peace of mind and good health. It's a journey that anyone can take with a first step and for me, the journey began about ten years ago.

Ten years ago, I was a very different person to the one writing this book and never dreaming of writing a book. What would I write? Who for? And, frankly, who would be interested anyway?

I was leading a very "normal" life, as defined by our society, with a successful steady career ahead of me in local government as an education officer.

I had no real beliefs in anything of a spiritual nature and I was certainly not religious. After 30 years of service I was ingrained in the good old 9-to-5.

Today, ten years on, I am now a "hands on" healer helping people in any way I can and advising them on their own personal journey as a part of their overall healing process.

Yes Healing!
My journey led me to become a Reiki healer and the delightful ability to aid those in need.
I spend a great deal of time talking to my clients about many of the themes described in this book. Very often a new client will feel better after simply listening for ten minutes to what I tell them, before any physical healing even begins.

That's how powerful this stuff is!

For those who may not have been introduced to or experienced the true healing benefits of Reiki, (either personally or through friends, relatives, acquaintances), Reiki is a form of alternative medicine originating in Japan. Reiki practitioners use techniques of hands-on-healing with universal energy.

The healing serves both physical and emotional well-being.

I cannot express enough the many, many people who I, or other practitioners, have helped on their own personal journeys to good health, peace and happiness.

My journey began in a dark place but having "retired" from the 9-to-5, I began to truly understand and appreciate the power from within that is available to everybody, not just a chosen few.

With freedom from my previous day-to-day employment, I became invigorated and evolved into a hands-on healer and seeing the results of the healing is simply the best feeling in the world.

I also found time to embrace my lifelong passion for song writing and my musical journey complements the healing.

My songs draw on the themes and messages of my healing and personal journey experiences.

The ideas and experiences presented here may be challenging to you, some you may struggle to believe, or even appear incredulous, but I assure you they are all *my* truth.

They are how I reached this point in my life and how I now see the world very differently indeed and over the last 10 years they haven't failed me to date.

Of course, that doesn't mean that you have to agree with or believe everything, or indeed anything I say.

I always find it amazing that those who have first-hand experiences become believers and advocates. Yet some people will always doubt – and that is fine too. I can only provide the message and be a channel for the message and the healing.
How far each person accesses the individual power within them has to be *their* own personal journey.

When I'm sharing these ideas in person with clients who visit me for healing, I encourage them to challenge me, to find their own truths, to take on board what feels right for them and to leave the rest aside.

Without exception, they *all* come back for more so I must be doing something right!
You won't find loads of statistics in here, "proving" what I'm saying is correct.

This is a deliberate omission.

The internet is awash with statistics, but for every set of figures demonstrating one fact there is another "proving" the opposite. Statistics have become relatively meaningless, thanks largely to their abuse by politicians and others, desperate to convince us of their arguments, so instead I have avoided them.

I believe in any case that the truth speaks for itself and there is no need to try to prove what you are saying if it has a divine source.

If you, the reader, are ready to listen then you will hear.

You will also find only a very few references here to what might be called "the dark side" of life; "conspiracy" theories, corruption at the highest levels, government and corporate "fake news", alien interference and so on.

That's not because many of them aren't true…. whatever you believe! *It's because this book is about the light, not the dark.*

There are plenty of books available on those subjects and some are very well researched. The problem is that, the more people focus on the dark, the more they will help to create or prolong negativity in all its forms in the three-dimensional world that we call home.

What you focus on with your mind you get more of, as you will shortly read about.
Remember that tried and trusted phrase about the glass being half full.
So, let's focus on positivity, peace, happiness, abundance and health and all the good things that life has to offer. This all sounds a bit heavy. Well, maybe it is but we're going to smile and laugh with it too.

Life is meant to be fun, not deadly serious, as I hope to show you. We're going to look at how to be happy, how to find peace and how to be healthy.
Each of these are wholly interconnected and cannot really be separated. It is difficult to be truly happy (but not impossible) if, for example, you are in constant pain from an illness.

In reality *everything* and *everyone* is connected to *everyone* and *everything* else as we will discuss later.

Nevertheless, this division is a useful way of summarising the material in a user-friendly way throughout this text.

The first chapter will set the scene for the whole book. You will read about the amazing experiences I went through several years ago which transformed my fairly ordinary life into an extraordinary journey of spiritual discovery that is still unfolding every magical day.

The subsequent chapters then provide details of the things I've learned since then, or been shown to be strictly accurate, which you can use to bring all the positive things you desire into your own life.

From my journey, I will include my personal insight to:

- The Power of the Mind,
- Reiki & Healing,
- Life's Purpose,
- The Law of Attraction,
- Reincarnation,
- Religion, God, Angels,
- Coincidences, (Tip: No such thing!)
- Music & Frequency manipulation,
- Politics, Conspiracy Theories and even Global Warming!

My aim is simply to give you the insight and tools to transform your life into whatever you want it to be. The choice is always yours though. If certain things don't resonate with you then simply move on and take what does work for you.
If, for example, you find my views on Religion and/or God challenging, that's fine. You don't have to agree. As the comedian Dave Allen said, "May your God go with you".

At the end of each chapter you will find some practical suggestions for you to put the ideas presented into practice in your own life.
Try them out and be prepared to witness your own miracles!

Are you ready to start **YOUR** Journey?

1. "You've had a breakdown!"

I thought long and hard about how much detail to include in this book about the experience I had when I "woke up" to what is really going on in the world and beyond, my "spiritual awakening" if you like.

You may find some of it difficult to accept, I certainly did and so did my family and friends.

In the end I have decided to tell the story accurately, as it contains so many of the truths included here in this book and I know it is the absolute truth, so it will be powerful.
Why do you think politicians need spin doctors, whips and media consultants to support them?

If they spoke the truth none of them would be required because the truth is far more powerful than any lie will ever be. It is also quite difficult to challenge the truth as there is always a ready answer.

I hope the story below will show you where this book and its contents have come from and how life can totally surprise you at any moment.

So here we go.
I've only included the most important bits of the story which are those that relate directly to what this book is about.

It's about 9 or 10 years ago. I am happily married to my beautiful wife Caroline with two children, working in local government with a well-paid career, nice car etc. I am "living the dream". Or not.

I can't help feeling that something isn't right - I don't feel happy at work, in fact I'm starting to really dislike it, but I don't know why.

I have nice colleagues and a good boss, but I just have this feeling that I've taken a wrong turning somewhere and something is going to happen soon which will change my life forever.

It's the August Bank Holiday week-end and it's Friday evening. I'm playing with my band at a local pub called "The Swan".

Tomorrow I am heading to Liverpool with a group of friends for the annual Beatles festival. We have been many times before and have always enjoyed it, listening to Beatles bands from all around the world and staying in the Adelphi hotel.

Little do I know that my world is about to be turned upside down.

We are playing our set of cover songs to a crowd of about 100 people and suddenly strange things start to happen to me. We are playing a Beatles song and I can "feel" John Lennon singing with me.

What a coincidence you may think!

It's as if he is inside my head- that's the only way I can describe it. It's as if he and I are one person.

I've played hundreds of gigs previously and have never had anything like this happen before. My guitar doesn't sound right either- it's a Fender Telecaster but it sounds more like a jangly 1960s Rickenbacker which was the guitar that John used to play.

Looking around me I see that no-one else seems to have noticed anything out of the ordinary, so I keep it to myself. We finish our set with "Angels" by Robbie Williams and I have another weird experience.
I can see Robbie standing right in front of me and I can feel a real connection with him on a spiritual level.

Of course, no-one else saw him as he wasn't really there, so when I told them later that he was in the pub they obviously thought I'd lost my marbles, particularly as I went charging around trying to find him again.

I learned later that there is no time or space in the higher spiritual planes where these images come from so, I could have been viewing something that will happen at some point in the future, as we understand time on planet Earth.

It hasn't happened yet but I'm sure it will.

We head home and my wife is very worried about me due to my strange behaviour which is totally out of character.

The last word to describe me at that time was strange! I was usually Mr Normal!

Despite the strange events of Friday evening, she allows me to set off for Liverpool the next day as my good friend Steve has promised to look after me should anything else of a similar nature happen. I can't explain it, but I have a sense of something hugely significant in my life about to happen and I am in a state of anticipation.

At first everything in Liverpool appears normal, we are outside listening to one of the bands on an outdoor stage with hundreds of people milling about.
Then suddenly from nowhere there's a voice in my head; "Hello Keith. It's time to wake up now."
I look around but it's obvious that no-one else has heard it. I'm not really surprised at that because again I "felt" the voice in my head rather than heard it through my ears.

How do you feel a voice? There aren't really words to describe it. It then "speaks" again.
"Time to wake up as we agreed." I'm already awake, I think, or am I dreaming?

I have no idea what's going on and I notice the world is looking rather different. It's a bit like looking through a distorting mirror at the funfair, with blurred outlines and faces.

As the blurred image slowly clears it dawns on me that I am perhaps, being given a glimpse of what is happening behind the scenes of a three-dimensional world.

There are what I think are angels on the street, helping people. The sky has turned orange and I notice the song "Spirit in the Sky" is coming from the stage.

By now my friends have noticed I am acting totally out of character, staring into space, and they are clearly starting to get more than a bit worried about me.
Maybe they think someone has spiked my drink? The voice is "speaking" to me again.
"Keith, you are not who you think you are. You have much work to do."

You might imagine that this experience, whatever it is, would be frightening or at least unsettling. But no. A feeling of euphoria is sweeping over me as I begin to grasp that my life is about to change forever and my feelings of dissatisfaction with my current life have been preparing me exactly for this moment.
We wander around Liverpool, with my friends keeping a close eye on me and the voice keeps talking to me.

Eventually we head back to the Adelphi and I spot a disabled girl in a wheelchair in the foyer.
"Go and give her some healing." the voice tells me.

I have no idea how to give somebody healing, but I feel compelled to go over to her as instructed. I say "hello" and she looks at me warily before disappearing off to make her escape. I can't help feeling sad that I couldn't do anything to help her and she obviously thought I was a nutter!

Later in the evening we are out in the streets of Liverpool again and we come across some homeless guys outside the hotel.

I feel that I have to give them some money - I can't remember how much, but it wasn't just loose change, maybe about £40?

By this time my friends are really worried about me and they decide it is time I was taken back home where I can access the professional help I clearly need.
This is what eventually happens later that night and I end up at home in bed alone the following morning. As I'm lying there having woken up, the voice returns;
"You have a choice to make. You can return home now or carry on with the mission you took on before you came to Earth."

I assume by returning home the voice means leaving this physical life and heading back to the spirit world, where we come from? I'm not ready for that I decide, so I say I'm stopping here thank-you.

I have no idea what the "mission" is.

"Your friends are downstairs. When you go down in a moment, they will tell you that you've had a breakdown and not to worry as they will get you all the professional help you need. You are to go along with their diagnosis and agree to do what they suggest, even though you haven't had a breakdown.

You may even believe them for a short while. It doesn't matter. All will be well. You are not to return to your job. You will take early retirement. It will be arranged for you. I am leaving you now for a while but understand that I will return when the time is right."
Immediately, the room is filled with a wind-like energy which surrounds me and then disappears out the bedroom door in a rush.

All is quiet and I feel strangely content and at total peace.

The voice has gone. I lie there for a while thinking it all over and then wander downstairs. Our friends Steve and Karen are in the kitchen talking to my wife. Steve turns to me with a concerned expression as I enter.

"Hi Keith. I want you to listen carefully. You've had a breakdown but there's nothing to worry about. We will get you the help you need. "
"Thanks Steve. I'm ready now to accept help." I reply, smiling inside as it plays out exactly as I was told it would.

They take me to the local hospital where I'm seen by a consultant who questions me and decides I've had a breakdown and prescribes Valium for me. We head home again.

Over the next two weeks I'm visited several times by the team who look after people suffering from depression. All the time I'm feeling elated, rather than depressed and I only pretend to take the Valium to keep them happy, but I know I don't need to, so I dispose of it secretly.
After a few weeks I'm largely left alone, signed off sick from work by the doctor, although I've never once said I'm ill. That decision has been made for me. The voice has been silent all this time, but I did have a further spiritual experience of sorts.

One morning I walked down to the local shop to buy some milk. It was a beautiful sunny morning with barely a cloud in the sky. I thought to myself wouldn't it be great if I could be shown a sign to prove I was on the right track, just to underline my faith in what I'd seen and experienced and that I hadn't somehow imagined it all? I looked up into the sky and a lone cloud had appeared above me and it had a vaguely angelic shape but disappointingly wasn't particularly impressive.

"Hmm. Is that the best you can do?!" I said to nobody in particular and went into the shop.

When I came out 5 minutes later, I glanced up and there was a perfectly shaped angel cloud right above me, in perfect detail.
"Wow! Okay I'm now impressed!"

Not only that, as I walked back up the road, the angel cloud followed me all the way, maintaining its perfect shape.

I reached home and the cloud sat above our house for the next few minutes until it eventually disappeared. I knew this was a clear sign to me that things were progressing according to plan, although I still didn't know what the plan was.

After a few months I start to think about going back to work, but every time I consider it, I feel that it's the wrong thing for me. It's not what I'm meant to do.
I remember what the voice said to me. I arrange to see my boss to decide my future. He listens sympathetically but tells me there is absolutely no chance of early retirement whatsoever. I go back home disappointed.

We have a few similar meetings with my boss, the Union representative, Personnel and Occupational Health but there is absolutely no movement. They all say I have no chance of being granted early retirement and that I should return to work once I am "better". I think about going back to work after Christmas.

Christmas comes and goes, and I still don't feel right about it, so I don't go back. I decide that if I can't have early retirement, I'll just leave and find something else to do. This is quite a big decision as it is a very well-paid job and I have only ever worked in local government so I have no idea what I might do instead.

A few more weeks pass, and nothing happens. I'm about to resign from my job and plunge into the unknown when I get a phone call completely out of the blue from Personnel asking if I'm still interested in accepting early retirement. Yes, yes, of course I am!

I end up signing the relevant papers the day before the deadline for applications, but it's approved. I'm free. Just as the voice predicted. I shouldn't have doubted - lesson number one. It's a great feeling.

Now what?

Still no voice.

I start doing a bit of gardening for the neighbours and it soon snowballs into a job for the time being. It's great being outdoors after sitting inside an office for 30 years and I meet some lovely people, but there's still something missing and I just know I should be doing something else, but what?
I'm about to find out.

A few months later, I am standing in a queue at the National Exhibition Centre near Birmingham waiting to go into a music event. I get chatting to a guy in the queue next to me who, it turns out, is a doctor. We talk about music, guitars and such like and then totally out of the blue he asks;
"Do you do Reiki?"
"No."
"You need to. Find a teacher to show you how."

Well, the music event was pretty poor, and I headed home. I thought about what he'd said on and off over the next few weeks. I'd heard of Reiki, but I wasn't sure what it was, but I knew someone whose partner did something with Reiki so I went to see her to see if she could train me. She wasn't a Reiki master, so she couldn't offer training, but she put me onto her teacher who could. And that's how I got started.
Hello and Welcome to Reiki!

My good friend Bernie took me under her wing and taught me Reiki levels 1, 2 and 3 over the following three years. I started to do healing on family and friends, and it grew from there.
I have since developed my own approach to healing and most days now I am either giving hands-on healing and / or sending healing to clients and I absolutely love what I do.

I have witnessed some amazing results with healing, and I have also experienced deep sadness when a terminally ill client leaves this life. More about this later.

But what about the voice?

Well, it was about a year after the Liverpool experience that it reappeared. To be honest, I was starting to wonder if I had somehow dreamt the whole thing or got it completely wrong.

When it did come back, I was ready for it, though, and it was a very controlled experience. In fact, nobody knew that I was going through it this time as it was very measured, and I was able to behave normally throughout, so no-one suspected.

It wasn't a voice though - it was more of a feeling, a knowingness. I can't describe it, but I just *knew.*

I've since learned that as you climb the ladder or ascend to spiritual enlightenment you leave voices and words behind as they are unreliable and easily misinterpreted. Instead, as we will see in the next chapter, your feelings never lie so they are used as one of the main vehicles for communication until you reach an advanced level of consciousness.

Anyway, I was "told" that all was going to plan, and I was doing fine. I then was given a glimpse into enhanced consciousness for a few hours and it was mind-blowing!

What does that really mean? I will try to explain.

Back in the days of Atlantis (yes, it really did exist), people had far greater consciousness than we do nowadays. They could interact fully with plants and animals. They could hear flowers growing, for example.

With the fall of Atlantis (which became the Biblical story of the flood) humans lost those powers and we have been working towards their reappearance ever since.

I was suddenly far more aware of what was going on around me than ever before. I knew who that person driving towards me was and I knew why they were there, even though they were complete strangers. I knew why that dog over there was crossing the road. I knew why that leaf had just fallen from that tree and I glimpsed the inter-connectedness of it all!

It didn't last long, but I can still remember it vividly. It isn't possible to live like that within current human society, of course, so I wasn't unhappy to return to "normal" (whatever that is!) but I remain immensely grateful for having experienced it. It was like viewing the world through God's eyes.

Again, it's very difficult to do justice to this experience as it goes way beyond words, but I felt I just knew and connected with *everything*.

Shortly after this experience I was walking down by our local canal, thinking how much I'd learned since my life as a local government officer had terminated, and a canal barge came past with the unlikely name of "Tooksomegetting" which made me laugh as I knew it was referring to me.

Reading this through now it all looks nice and easy. That happened, then this, then we all lived happily ever after.
That's not even close to the truth, however.

No-one has ever said that the spiritual path is an easy option and I have to agree with that. Despite what I was feeling inside (joy, peace, elation etc) at the time, I also was faced with watching my family and friends suffer as they were convinced I had suffered a serious mental breakdown. I decided I couldn't tell them what had really happened as it would worry them even more, so I kept it all to myself.
It was like living two lives.

On the inside, despite the occasional doubts, I knew really that I was perfectly sane and facing the greatest adventure of my life.

On the outside I had to play along with the world's view of me as somebody who'd lost the plot. It was made worse by the fact that when you wake up to the real truth you really want your family and friends to find it too.

I also had to go through this charade with the mental health professionals who were sent to look after me.

They were all lovely people, but I kept thinking what a waste of time and resources this was, that could be put to much better use elsewhere. It wasn't easy, but I kept it to myself for several years before I ventured to start telling my family and friends what had really happened that day in Liverpool.

By then people were coming to me regularly for healing and it was much easier for them to at least begin to understand what I'd been through and to at least partly accept what I was saying, as they could see the positive results people were clearly achieving from the healing. It still took years for them to come to terms with it fully though.

I also went through periods of time when I too had a few doubts as to my version of the story.

My biggest issue was that, if I really was here to help people to move on, to offer healing and to show them the way to enlightenment, why hadn't I had any vague notion of this for the first 50 years of my life?

The answer soon started to present itself.

I started to understand that I had chosen to live the first half of my life "asleep" so that I could then empathise with people who were still asleep when they came to me for help. I could fully understand how they were feeling because I'd been there myself.

Experience is powerful, hence the purpose of life on earth.

I was also told that my experience in Liverpool was what is commonly called a "walk in" by spiritualists. This is when another soul or another part of your own soul literally "walks into" and replaces or joins with the original soul attached to your body.

In my case, a part of my higher self, entered my being to raise my consciousness to the level needed for the next stage of my life journey.

To the outside World I still looked the same, but inside I knew I was very different.
I was also concerned that I really didn't have all the answers to the questions I was receiving from clients.

Amazingly, though, I found that I was giving answers that I didn't realise I knew. The right answer was being given to me. I didn't have to think about it.
I also began to see how my life path had brought me to this place.

I had a happy childhood with lots of friends until the day I passed the eleven plus exam to go to the local grammar school. As most of my existing friends in the immediate neighbourhood went to the local secondary modern school, I was immediately ostracised and lost many of those good friends. I got used to the name-calling after a while, but it did hurt at the time. We know kids can be cruel.

Of course, this was all designed to prepare me for my isolation forty years later when I woke up spiritually speaking!
So, there it is. That was my "breakdown" experience and the beginning of the next stage of my life as a healer. I will never forget it.

Once you wake up there is no going back!

Do try this at home:

Give some thought to how happy you are in your current life.
Are you excited and passionate about your life or career?
If you are, then that's great. You are clearly on the right path for you.

If not, what would you like to do for a living instead? Don't worry about practicalities at this stage, just imagine waking up each Monday morning and being excited that it's a working day.

If you're not sure, try starting with a favourite hobby. Hold on to whatever thoughts you have for your new career for the time being. We will come back to them a little later on.

2.   Trust your feelings!

My journey described in the previous chapter involved some pretty difficult personal decisions.

I was giving up a very good salary and had a mortgage and family to support. Saying goodbye to most of that income with a reduced pension was a challenge, but despite what everybody thought, I knew it was the right thing to do because I ignored the fear that my mind was creating and instead trusted my feelings on the matter.

In this chapter we're going to look at how useful your feelings are when confronted with life choices.

Everyday life gets more and more complex.

When I was growing up you had a choice of tea or coffee to drink, if you were lucky. Nowadays we are literally spoiled for choice - latte, mocha, Americano, expresso, cappuccino, decaf, one shot or two, semi-skimmed, full cream, soya, flat white etc etc.

Turn on the TV and you have a ridiculous number of channels to choose from (most of which are continually pumping out the same dross over and over again).
Life can be very confusing with so many choices confronting us.

Don't you sometimes wish you had a personal life coach on hand to guide you through the difficult decisions you have to make on a daily basis?

- Someone who knows what's best for you, always has your best interests at heart, has no hidden agenda and never makes a mistake?
- Someone who isn't swayed by fashion or the latest trend or fad.
- Someone who doesn't listen to gossip and is truly your best friend?

Good news! You do, but you won't find them on Facebook. You have an in-built satellite navigation system called your feelings.

How many people do you know who get married, then a few years later get divorced, saying "I knew he / she was the wrong one as I stood there in the church, but I thought it was too late to stop it."

In other words, they let their head (the conscious mind which said "you can't possibly back out now - it's far too late!") overrule their feelings, which come from the sub-conscious and unconscious minds which were only looking out for you by making you feel uncomfortable as they knew that your choice of partner would not bring you happiness.

Let's have a quick look at the mind as it was first described by Sigmund Freud so that we can better understand what's really going on.
In his model the human mind is split into 3 parts:

- the conscious,
- the sub-conscious and
- the unconscious.

The **conscious mind** or the ego is what you use all day long.
If someone asks you "What's two plus two?" your conscious mind leaps into action, says "I know!" and gives the right answer, unless you are as poor at maths as I am. It interacts with the world at large through the senses - speech, sight, hearing, touch and smell and it firmly believes it is "you".

It isn't you.

It's only a part of you, the part that interacts with the physical world. It's the part of you that your friends and family think of as "you" and very often the part that you also think is the whole "you" because that's what the world tells you.

But it's not.

The ego likes you to think that it's you because, if it's not you, then it doesn't exist (because it's nobody else) and it can't bear that thought, so it does its best to convince you that this is all you are.

The **subconscious mind** is the powerhouse that works largely behind the scenes.
It handles all the bodily processes we all need to stay alive, so you don't have to use your conscious mind to think "I need to breathe in now." or "I need to pump extra blood into my abdomen." as it happens "automatically".

It also houses all of our most recent memories.

The **unconscious mind** is where we store all the past experiences gained in our life (and previous lives). It is talking to the conscious mind all the time through the sub-conscious and it uses emotions and feelings to get its message across.

Freud's definitions have been disputed by psychologists since his time and the super-conscious and supra-conscious have since been "discovered". However, this simple three-part "mind" will suffice for our purpose here in this chapter.

The important point to understand is that our feelings, intuition, instinct etc come from a much more reliable source than do our thoughts.
Why?

Well, our thoughts come from our conscious mind, which not only thinks it is all you are (major mistake) and so has a very distorted view of reality, but which has also been continuously conditioned by the media and the world at large since the day you were born.

Turn the TV on and you will immediately witness the brainwashing at work. Constant adverts tell you that you need to buy the latest phone or the most powerful car or this brand of soap powder to make your life fully complete and joyful.

If you're a young male don't expect women to come flocking to you unless you are sporting the very latest aftershave produced by an exotic sounding company with a French name that probably doesn't even exist.

It's all utter nonsense, of course, no sooner have you purchased such products than the adverts appear for the next model or brand which supersedes what you've just bought telling you your life can't possibly be complete without this latest offering....and on and on it goes in a never-ending cycle of consumerism.

People queue up at midnight to buy the latest smart phone which does virtually the same things as the one they already own but has a different name or model number. Nowhere is the insanity of this process more evident than at Christmas which has become a ludicrous exercise in commercialism which sadly bankrupts many families for a large part of the ensuing year.

It's all nonsense but that's how powerful this stuff is in getting you to part with your money.

A process of buying things you don't need, with credit card money you don't really have!

Despite their many differences, every world religion tells you that happiness does not come from having more or bigger or better "things", but it comes from finding your peace internally, not through accumulating more things externally.

That's why you see so many celebrities, who on the surface "have it all", languishing in therapy. They have the money, the mansion, the fame, the cars, the "perfect" partner and they are utterly miserable. The so-called American dream is all-to-often in reality, a living nightmare.

But it's not just adverts that brainwash you, many programmes do the same. Soap operas are designed to depress the viewer. Watch five minutes of EastEnders' misery and I guarantee you will feel worse because of the storyline. Why do they want to keep you depressed?

Several reasons, including if you are down you are unlikely to challenge anything going on in the world and also you are even more likely to seek solace by purchasing more stuff, you don't need or really want, thereby filling the corporate pockets even more!

Why do you think they are called television programmes? The clue is in the name – they are literally "programming" you with negativity!

It's not just the media that is corrupting the conscious mind in this way. Look at the education system in England.

At an increasingly early age children are subjected to a range of tests designed to measure their so-called intelligence. From those results those who don't fare very well are then conditioned into thinking that they are inferior to their peers and their career options are then severely limited to the more menial tasks.

Their self-esteem suffers and some may eventually turn to artificial stimulants (drink, drugs etc) as a way of coping. And the system has the audacity to claim that school days "are the best years of your life."
Youngsters are told they are the wrong height, the wrong shape, too fat, too thin, the wrong colour, not wearing the "right" designer clothing, come from the wrong family and so on.

More recently, this is reinforced 24/7 via social media through peer group pressure and so-called trolls who are the internet's equivalent to the school bully.

Women have a really tough time in my opinion (nothing new there). Their magazines are filled with air-brushed photos of impossibly beautiful and shapely women who don't really exist. Fashion dictates what they are supposed to wear, including "killer" high heels that wreck their feet (the clue is in the name), and how they are supposed to look.

This is the power of the media.

If you want a really good example of how your mind is tossed from pillar to post just look at the issue of healthy eating.

Virtually everything we eat has at some point been branded as bad for us by the media. Many of those so-called "bad" foods have also at some point been labelled as good for us. Foodstuffs seesaw between the two camps regularly.
I remember in the 1970s when margarine was held up as the new healthy alternative to full fat butter. Now it's gone back the other way. For every article declaring the positive health benefits of drinking a glass of red wine daily, there is another telling us about the damage it leads to.

Coconut oil. Good or bad? You can find articles both for and against. How on earth do you know what is the truth?

This is the kind of nonsense our poor conscious mind has to contend with on a daily basis. No wonder it's so screwed up. If you only use your thoughts to guide you in your life choices, you are likely to come unstuck because this is the type of contradictory garbage the conscious mind has to wade through in order to attempt to give you an answer.

Fortunately, help is at hand.
The unconscious and sub-conscious do not suffer from the same abuse.
They are immune to the effects of the outside world's conditioning. They have the answers you need to all life's questions and are there to provide the answers for you. They do this via your feelings, not your thoughts.

Here's an example: You've been offered a new job and it means relocating to another town. You're not sure what to do. Your head (conscious mind) is filled with conflicting thoughts...
"It's a great opportunity- I should take it."
"But it means uprooting the family and they are all settled here."
"I'm getting on a bit - it's now or never. I won't get this chance again."

"I'm comfortable in my current job. Do I really want the added pressure?"

"I'm not sure I'm good enough for this promotion."

"What if they see through me?"

"I could buy that new BMW with the extra salary I'll be getting."

"It would look really good on my CV for the future."

"I'll be earning more than my brother and he's more qualified."

And so on and so on...

These thoughts are, of course, influenced by the conditioning outlined above so inevitably they are in a state of constant turmoil. There is no definitive clear answer to the question should I take this job or not?

The answer you are looking for is to be found in your feelings, not your thoughts.

Feelings are the language of the soul.

Have you ever walked into a room and felt instantly uncomfortable with someone there who you've never met before?

You can't put your finger on it, but it just doesn't feel right? That's your internal sat nav telling you that this person isn't good for you for whatever reason and you are best avoiding them.

Maybe you've been driving down a road and felt you needed to turn off and go home a different route to your normal one? When you get home, you find there was a crash on the road you left which you avoided.

That's your feelings guiding you. They are doing this all the time, but the trouble is most people either don't notice or choose to ignore them and use their head to decide what to do.

You are looking for a new home and you've visited dozens, but none has really appealed to you. Suddenly, you walk into one and it just *feels* right. You just know it's the one for you and you have to buy it. It proves to be an excellent choice and you have many happy years there. Thanks to your feelings.

Let's be clear, there is no "right" or "wrong" answer to the question should you take the job or not.

You can choose either and the world will continue to turn. However, one answer will lead you to a more positive and happier outcome than the other. Why? Because it is more in line with your life's purpose.

My life has a purpose? Wow! That's good news! How do I find out what it is?

Only you know what that purpose is. You decided before you arrived on Earth. Generally speaking, though, every person is here to remember who they really are by progressing spiritually. As you go through life your feelings will tell you whether you are on the right path for you or not.

Maybe this is not the first time you have felt the need to change direction. That's your feelings telling you to make a change in order to follow the path most in tune with your life's purpose.

Let's assume that you chose to work on greed.
Life will continue to present you with experiences from which you will gain an insight into greed until you've learned all there is to learn.

In our example above, this new job might, for example, offer a significant hike in your salary (so you could buy more things you don't need), thereby enticing you to take it, but the fall-out might be an unhappy partner who has to leave his / her current job where they are happy and this might lead to a breakdown in your relationship.

Alternatively, you could find if you turned it down your partner might resent it later on when you are made redundant from your previous job and you are faced with losing your home or relying solely on your partner's salary to survive.

So, you have to make a choice.

One choice will eventually lead to a more positive outcome than the other and this will, of course, vary from person to person dependent upon their individual circumstances. For some the "right" decision will be to take the job, for others it will be the "wrong" choice.

So how on earth do you choose?

With your feelings!

Imagine yourself taking the job. How does it feel? Close your eyes and live it as if it's really happening now. See yourself walking into your new work-place to meet your new colleagues and sitting at your new desk.

How does it feel?

Does it feel good or is there something that doesn't feel quite right? Where do you normally feel things? For many people it's in their stomach or their gut, so when asked how they made the "right" choice people often say; "I just had a gut feeling about it."

Wherever you normally feel things, that's the place to focus on. If you can't decide where that place is in your body, just go with your general feeling overall. Is it positive or negative? Now imagine yourself not taking the job and staying where you are. How does that feel?
Compare the two feelings.

One will *feel* better than the other and whichever that is will be the better course of action for you to take. You can, of course, over-ride your feelings and choose the other option as you have complete free will in everything you do. Rest assured, though, that in doing so you are choosing the long and winding road route instead of the easier path.
That's okay if you want to experience the more difficult path, but if you want the easier route then follow your feelings. It's your choice. So that's how you do it.

Your feelings never tell you anything but the truth.

They are not influenced by thoughts, like the conscious mind, but instead they are hard-wired to offer you the best guidance available.

That guidance takes full account of your life purpose that you signed up to before incarnating or starting your journey (which you've probably forgotten now you're here).

That's why it is always "right".

Don't be afraid to use it and transform your life!

Do try this at home:

Think of a time when your life reached a crossroads and you had to decide which direction to take.

Did you follow your feelings or your head?

How did it work out for you?

Whenever you are given a choice in life from now on, try to tune in to your feelings before making your final decision, using the method shown in this chapter.

After a while it will become second nature and life will seem much easier.

3. Believing is seeing!

Now you understand how to make choices in your life by using your feelings, let's turn to look at the incredible power that you hold in your mind.
This is truly life-changing once you understand and begin to use the principles which I have summarised in this chapter.

"Believing is seeing!" is the title of one of my band's songs and, no it's not the wrong way around.

So many of our well-known sayings have deep and meaningful truths embedded in them, such as "go with the flow" or "be careful what you wish for", but sometimes they have been twisted out of shape like Chinese whispers. This is one of those.

"I'll believe it when I see it" is probably a version you have used yourself on more than one occasion.

The trouble is, that is actually a negative statement which really means, "I won't believe it until I see it." or "I don't believe it will happen so go ahead and be stupid enough to try to prove me wrong!"

If we are going to enjoy our time on earth, we don't want negativity, we want positivity, so read on and learn how to change your life for the better.

Perhaps you have heard of the **Law of Attraction**? There are plenty of books out there on the subject.

In brief, your mind is immensely more powerful than most people realise. It is busy creating everything that happens to you all the time you are awake.

To be more accurate, it is co-creating with everyone else on the planet, but *you* are the key player in the events that make up your individual life experience.

Other people's thoughts, actions and deeds do affect your life, of course, but you have the casting vote on how you will choose to *respond* to them.

How you choose to respond has an enormous impact on your subsequent life experiences including your happiness, health and peace, as we will see.

The majority of the population still believe that life "happens" to them through a random sequence of events, coincidences or synchronicities that they are relatively powerless to influence, so they see themselves as victims of fate, chance, bad luck, faulty genes, the wrong Government etc.

This viewpoint is reinforced continuously by the media who delight in reporting (or making up) bad news stories. The truth is that this is simply not the case. You are not a victim. You are a creator!

You are the prime creator of your own life.

Every second that you are awake your mind is sending out **thought vibrations** which are creating your tomorrows.

Yes – Your mind is creating your future!

I tell my clients to imagine that the universe is a photocopier, sending back multiple copies of your thought creations to you until eventually they manifest in the physical world that we call reality.

Look around the room you are in. Everything there started from a thought. Somebody thought it would be a good idea to have something to sit on, or to write with, or to keep warm with etc. Having drawn up an initial design, tried out a prototype or two, their original thoughts / ideas eventually became actual "things" in our world.

It is exactly the same process with your own day to day thoughts.

If you keep thinking something it will eventually appear in your life, whether you want it to or not.

This is what John Lennon was referring to in the song "Nowhere Man" when he said, "The world is at your command".

This is what I mean by "Believing is seeing". If you truly believe you can create something you will see it because it will show up in your life.

How does this work?

Well, you have to understand that everything that has ever existed or will ever exist in the future is already available in the universe. That's because there is no such thing as time, it's simply a human invention to help us to exist in some sort of order within the 3D world.

When you have an "idea", you are in effect choosing something from an existing selection. It's just that your idea hasn't yet appeared in physical form on this planet. It's like standing in front of the biggest video library shelf you can imagine, looking at all of the options stacked there and saying, "I'll have that one."

Once you understand the power of your mind you can use it to attract to you anything you want, almost without exception.
This includes:

- financial abundance,
- health and wellbeing,
- the partner of your dreams,
- a new car or anything you fancy.

"Oh yeah? I'll believe it when I see it!" I hear you say without a trace of irony.
Well, the truth is that, if that is how you think, you will probably never see it.
If you are thinking negative thoughts such as "I don't have enough money for a new car", that thought gets "photocopied" and sent back to you, so in essence you are now less likely to attract the funds you need to buy the car.

Every time you repeat that negative thought you are increasing the likelihood of never having enough funds for a car.

The same is true in relation to your health.
We all know someone who goes around saying "I get a cold every winter without fail. Why me?" Sure enough, a few weeks into winter that same person comes down with a cold and takes great delight in saying "I told you so."

What he / she doesn't realise is that they have helped to attract the cold to themselves by continuously sending out a negative thought vibration to which the universe has to respond.

That's how it's wired up - to give you what you are focusing your thoughts on. Your thoughts create your life.
The thoughts you are having today are creating tomorrow's experiences.
That's why man-flu is so much worse than a woman's cold- because men *think* it is!

Here's the good news.

Once you understand this, it's a relatively simple matter to change your thought patterns to predominantly positive ones and your life will begin to change as if by magic.

No, you don't have to be positive all of the time, I suggest you aim for about 80% and don't criticise yourself if you "fail" sometimes.
You are human, and all humans are imperfect. We are meant to be.

If you were perfect, there would be no point being on the planet as you would have nothing to experience and learn.

As you begin to see results, however, it will become an easier habit to remain positive than to be negative, until eventually it becomes your natural state.

It is in fact your natural state, the one you were born with, but the world has systematically beaten it out of you from day one by bombarding you with negativity via the media, the education system and even well-meaning members of your family who pass on to you what they themselves were conditioned into believing.

We will look at that another time - for now let's stay positive.

Back to the song title.

In order to attract anything into your life you have to have faith / belief that it will come.
In fact, you need to FEEL that it is already here, even though it isn't.

It's a bit like a "let's pretend" childhood game. All children are experts at pretending they are Princesses or Marvel Super-Heroes or Gender Neutral or whatever they like. Most adults lost that talent long ago, but it's actually very powerful.

Let's take the new car example.

Rather than thinking negative thoughts such as:
 "I need a new car.",
"My car is worn out.",
"I can't afford a new car.", instead think positive things such as:
"My new car is on its way to me.",
"I am so happy with my new car.",
"How grateful I am to be sent a new car." etc.

Feel excited and grateful at the thought of your new car which is even now on its way to you and it will eventually arrive. It has to, as I said before, that's how the universe is wired up.

"Ask and it is given." as someone who knew all this stuff two thousand years ago once said.
This is what Jesus meant when he said; "Knock and the door will be opened to you."

Don't ever focus on *how* it will come, just trust in the end result and leave the rest to the universe / God.

Focusing on "how" it will manifest shows that you do not have sufficient faith and that will hinder or at worst prevent the arrival of your request.

Jesus said to enter the kingdom of heaven you need to become like little children. This doesn't just mean being pure and innocent but also to have complete faith, trust and belief in your own abilities to manifest whatever you desire.

Children truly believe they can be or do anything, until the world tells them otherwise and they stop believing.

You need to have a similar child-like faith that you can manifest whatever you want, and it will eventually show up.

Let me share an example with you from my own life to demonstrate how this works.

I was sat talking with Jamie, who did most of the recording of our first CD, and we were discussing how to improve our recording experience. At the time we were using his old lap-top to run Logic music software, which only works on Apple computers.

Unfortunately, I only owned a PC.

We were deliberating on how much better it would be if I had an Apple computer myself to speed things along, rather than relying on a fairly old lap-top that kept letting us down.

"How much are they, Jamie?" I asked.

"You really want an iMac, and they're about £1700." he replied.

I didn't have that sort of money readily available, so I just said okay leave it with me.

Later that night I sat quietly and sent out gratitude for the iMac that I knew was coming to me. I truly believed that it would come.

I visualised the package arriving and me opening it.

Then I left it to the universe / God / creator / source to come good and I forgot about it.
Nothing happened at first….

But then about a week later I got a phone call from a friend who only rings me very rarely, asking if I could help him to fix his guitar. We got chatting and I asked him if he was recording these days and, if so, what was he using?

"I've got an iMac." he said. "They're brilliant."

I explained that I was on the look-out for one and his reply was;
"I know someone who's selling one. He's just bought a new one."
Well, I took his number and rang him up. Sure enough, he had just bought a new one and invited me to view the old one. It was just what I needed, and he let me have it for £500.

It "just happened" that I had a birthday coming up, so I managed to get some birthday money together to pay a deposit for it and he even let me pay the rest later.
Not only was I now the proud owner of an Apple computer, it also came with the Logic software we needed plus a whole load of other music stuff that has proved invaluable.

And that's not all…
The guy I bought it from (real name John, but I call him Tinkerbelle) is now one of the band, The Acoustic Rainbow, having done final mixing and sprinkling fairy dust (that's why!) on the first album.

All that from that one thought I sent out and one subsequent phone call.

Coincidence some of you may say. Well, when you've had a hundred similar "coincidences" as I have perhaps you will change your mind. We will look at some of them in a later chapter.

"Great! I can focus on winning the lottery and let the universe send me the right numbers!" you cry.
Hmmm. Not quite.

You see, you will find that it is much easier to manifest things that are of benefit to others, your local community or even the world in general, rather than simply for your own personal gain, like the lottery numbers. "That's not fair! You got a new Apple computer for yourself." I hear you reply.

That's true…. but my aim is / was to spread the words and music of healing as far as possible to help people.
It's not about becoming rich and famous.

When you genuinely want to help improve people's lives on the planet you unleash higher spiritual energies that make it much easier to manifest what you are asking for. This is because you are then acting in a truly God-like manner.
You don't have to believe me when I say I wasn't acting in my own interests as the proof is there in the awesome and rapid response from the universe in giving me exactly what I needed to make it happen.

Here are a few pointers about the process to ensure you get it right.

First, let's go back to the saying "be careful what you wish for".

Understand that you need to be careful with your thinking to avoid attracting what you don't want.

As a healer I am privileged to spend time with people suffering from all kinds of illness, including cancer. Some of those people are committed to beating the disease and say things like "I'm going to fight this cancer!"

At first this might look like a positive statement but remember that the universe will send you exactly what you are focused on. So, if you're thinking "I'm going to fight this cancer." the universe responds with "Have some more fighting cancer" which is of course the exact opposite of what the person really wants to attract.

Instead, I try to encourage these people to think "I am healthy." or "Thank you for sending me complete health and well-being." or something similar, even when they are desperately ill.

The universe then responds with "Have some more health." See the difference?

The first is focused on cancer (negative) and the second on health (positive).

It is a small but absolutely critical difference. **Don't ever focus on what you don't want**.

"I will not get a cold." is another similar example, as is "Please send me some money so I can pay my bills." Instead, say "I am full of health and vitality" or "Thank-you for sending me ample funds to pay my bills." and it is far more likely to work out fine.

A common question I get asked all the time is why then does God / the Universe send bad things to good people?

Surely, he / she / it knows people really want good things only, no matter what they are thinking?
The answer to this question is as follows. First, man has been granted the blessing of free will and nothing in this universe ever overrides that (it's not the case in other universes).
We are free to create whatever we desire, including things that we deem to be bad.

There is no vetting process from above. We can't have it both ways guys - complete freedom to create and also someone granting or denying our creations by running them past some sort of judgment criteria.

Secondly, there is no such process because at the highest spiritual level there is no such thing as good or bad as they are all just experiences and therefore equally valid in the human experience. This is why we are told by religions that our sins are forgiven.

There is really no such thing as sin, as everything is just an experience, so there is nothing to forgive. It goes back to Einstein and relativity - without cold the concept of heat is meaningless, or at best only theoretical, in other words we can't experience one without the other.

Similarly, health is not truly experienced without having its opposite to reference to, which is illness, both are required in order to experience life fully in the physical plane. To truly know what we wish to create we sometimes have to first experience things we don't enjoy so that we can then make the "right" or happier choice.

There's another aspect to this that requires explanation. How come someone gets cancer and they never thought it would happen to them? If thinking / the power of the mind is the main source of our experiences, where has it come from in this situation?

Well, sometimes the person may not be consciously thinking about illness, but subconsciously it may be ticking away continuously in the background. This is often the case if there is a so-called family history of cancer. In addition, we are all bombarded with images of cancer via the media.

It's on the TV.
It's in the newspapers.
It's all over the internet.

You can't get away from it. And it all seeps into the subconscious cumulatively. Not only that, but everything that happens to one person has some impact upon everyone else (and everything) on the planet, as we are all interconnected, so the more people thinking about cancer, the more widespread the effects.

The same is now happening with dementia which has become the latest illness the media is focused on. No surprise then that more people are now suffering from dementia than ever before.

What you focus on you get more of. What more people focus on, you get even more of. As a result, it is important to get into the habit of only thinking positively.

Turn off the TV news and ignore the media and your health will without doubt improve.

So that's what this 3-minute pop song is all about. Hold on to your belief about something you desire and you will see it eventually manifest in your life. Here endeth this lesson!

Do try this at home

Use the power of your mind to manifest something in your life. Start with something small so that you don't fall prey to not believing you can do it.

Use the method shown in this chapter. Thank the Universe or God for sending it you and truly feel that it is on its way to you.

Then sit back and wait. Don't give it another thought until it arrives.

As you gain in confidence and belief in your abilities, you can move on to bigger and greater manifestations such as your dream career.

4. When dreams are all you have, then you have everything

Now you know how to use the power of your mind to create the life you want, let's focus in on what you really *really* want, like the Spice Girls, and learn how to enhance your powers of manifesting to the next level.

The title of this chapter is the first line of the chorus of an **Acoustic Rainbow** song from our first album titled **"You are the Light of Love"**.

Like many of the band's songs, it's far from a throwaway line as it contains a message to guide the listener to a more fulfilling and joyful life.
That's what this book is all about too, of course, so let's take a closer look...

At first sight the chorus line may appear to be wrong. If all you've got is dreams then you ain't got very much, have you sunshine?! It reminds me of blues guitarist Seasick Steve's wonderful title "I started out with nothing and I've still got most of it left."

However, just like Steve's title, it is in fact a statement of positivity. Here's why.

As you know now, if you focus on your dream and keep visualising it happening then you are bringing it to you. If you can think positively about it most of the time it will eventually manifest in your life. What you focus on in your mind the universe will in time give you via the law of attraction, as discussed in the previous chapter, but which is so fundamental it is worth repeating here.

Look around the room you are in.

Remember, everything there started out as somebody's thought – the chair you're sitting on, the internet device you are using, the internet itself, the table you are sitting at and so on.

Everything came from an initial thought that somebody eventually changed into a physical thing. This is how the universe is wired up - to respond to thoughts (in truth it is made up of thoughts alone, but we won't get into that metaphysical stuff just yet).

So, it's very important to have a dream (a dream can be considered your ideal thought) and to revisit it often. As Richard Rogers wrote in the lyric for "Happy Talk" from the movie "South Pacific";

"You've got to have a dream, if you don't have a dream, how are you gonna have a dream come true?"

Precisely!

Even Captain Sensible understood it. Or did he? Anyway, a great time to do this is when you are about to fall asleep at night. As you are in that half-awake / half asleep moment, picture your dream in as much detail as possible and try to *feel* as if it has already materialised, then fall asleep.

Your subconscious mind will then carry on promoting your dream on your behalf while you are asleep.
It's like a freebie working on your behalf for 8 hours.

So, getting back to the song lyric, what this line is really saying is that, once you understand the principles of manifesting what you want in your life, then you can literally "dream" or think anything into existence.

- A new car,
- your ideal partner,
- more money,
- health and wellbeing,
- your dream kitchen and so on.

All can be acquired by the same method, so you truly do have access to everything (Does anybody really dream about kitchens?).

Anyway, sounds too good to be true?

Hopefully you have already tried this for yourself as suggested at the end of the previous chapter, starting with a relatively small request before you move up to larger manifestations.

The Universe / God doesn't differentiate between big and little requests, but your human mind does, so you are unlikely to have enough faith in the process to successfully manifest something big and impressive to begin with. Start with a small ask, for example, a certain type of flower or fruit to manifest, something that you don't normally have at home, so you will be suitably impressed when it arrives.

The most powerful way of asking for something is to say thank you for it before it arrives, for example, "Thank you for sending me a pink orchid. I am truly grateful." And to feel gratitude in your heart, as if it has already arrived. You only need to "ask" once and then hold onto a child-like belief that what you have asked for will appear.

No doubts just believe.

Your conscious mind will try to butt in with its normal take on things; "Don't be ridiculous, this is never going to work!" "Who taught you this rubbish?" etc.

Ignore it.

Eventually, after you have had some success with manifesting, it will give up and stop trying to sabotage your efforts.
Give yourself a couple of days to manifest your flower or fruit and see what happens.
Don't think about how it will appear, just have the belief that it will. It works.

I know because I use it all of the time.

For further guidance try reading *"The Secret" by Rhonda Byrne* as an easy introduction to this way of thinking or, for more advanced help I thoroughly recommend *"Ask and it is given" by Esther and Jerry Hicks.* It will change your life.

A friend of mine wanted to try this out for herself so I asked her to think of a flower that she wouldn't normally have around the house and ask it to appear. She chose an anemone. The next day I got an excited phone call from her…

"You'll never guess what's happened!"
"Go on, surprise me." I replied.

Well it turns out she had decided to do a bit of de-cluttering and was clearing out some old books in the spare bedroom. As she reached up to pick up some books from a shelf, she dropped one of them and it fell face open to the floor. The book was "A Guide to Wild Flowers of the British Isles" and you can guess which flower was featured on the page it had randomly opened to. That's right, a daisy!

Only kidding, of course it was the anemone! Okay, so she didn't have enough belief to manifest an actual anemone, but she did pretty well for a first attempt.

Another friend wanted to attract a partner into her life. I taught her the same procedure which she followed and even went so far as laying a place for him at the dinner table every evening, as if he had already shown up. It didn't take very long before he did, and they eventually got married.
Expressing gratitude is a very powerful activity, in fact it is the most effective form of prayer.

Many people pray for things to happen, "God, please send me enough money to pay my heating bill." for example.

This is not very effective because it's focused on the money not being there. It's focused on the present lack of money.

If the "prayer" is changed to "Thank you God for sending me enough money to pay my bills." it is focused on the money already being present and that is much more powerful.

If you wish for something to appear in your life, say thank-you and feel really grateful for it to hasten its appearance.
"When dreams are all you have, then you have everything." has another meaning too.

In our first interpretation the word "all" implies that you haven't got very much, as in "is that *all* you've got?" So, if you've only got dreams at first sight you don't have anything. You're still chasing rainbows. As shown above, this isn't the case, however.

Achieving any sort of success starts with having a dream, like Martin Luther King. However, the word "all" can also mean "everything", that is the opposite of its meaning in the first interpretation. So, this would translate into "when everything you have is seen to be a dream, then you have everything." This means when you realise that nothing in life is real (it's just a dream), then you have acquired spiritual mastery (you have everything).

This idea of life being an illusion and the universe a hologram is hardly a new concept, I should add, as it features in all of the main texts from the world's various religions albeit in the language of the time. John Lennon was also writing about this in "Strawberry Fields Forever" where "nothing is real".

More on this in a later chapter. It's even to be found in a well- known children's nursery rhyme...

Row row row your boat
Gently down the stream
Merrily merrily merrily merrily
Life is but a dream

In fact, this simple 4-line poem is an amazingly powerful little piece of spiritual writing that contains many universal truths.

Are you serious?

Absolutely. It's telling you to row your boat gently downstream in a joyful manner. Do not do the opposite – rowing hard against the current upstream - if you want a happy life.

The world is full of people doing just that – struggling against the flow of life and working far too hard at it to ever be happy. Life is meant to be joyful and relatively easy. There is no need to struggle if you go with the flow and believe.

Life is but a dream means it's all an illusion anyway, so stop taking it all so seriously and start enjoying it.

A useful image that I use when I explain the dream concept to my clients is that of a magician's show. Imagine you are in the audience as the magician prepares to do the famous sawing the woman in half routine. As you watch the saw cutting through the box where the woman's body is supposed to be, you don't get emotionally involved because you know that it's just a clever trick.

It's all just smoke and mirrors.

You may not know exactly how it's done (it's on the internet!), but you know it's fake as she is perfectly healthy and in one piece at the end of the performance. If, however, you thought that what you were experiencing was real and she was in real danger, then you would have a very different response to what you are witnessing - horror, shock, anger etc.

It's exactly the same principle with life on planet Earth, *but in reverse*. We believe that what we see, touch, smell, feel and hear is real so we do take it seriously.

We feel pain and joy, love and hate and every emotion in between which is *why* we are here - to experience life in all of its shapes and sizes. None of it is real, however, it is all a "trick", a "dream".

Everything is made of energy, even things that appear to be solid. Our eyes are calibrated to make things seem solid. We may think that we are tiny beings in an enormous universe, but the truth is that the universe only exists in our minds. We are creating our version of it with our thoughts. If we saw through this illusion, however, we wouldn't experience the full range of emotions, so it is presented to us as reality, until we learn to see through it as we grow spiritually over many lifetimes.

Pretty clever, eh? Well, what do you expect from God / the Universe? Would you believe that there is yet another sub-meaning in "When dreams are all you have...?"

Here goes. It kind of goes back to the song "Happy Talk".

One of my favourite authors, **Wayne Dyer**, said that we should try to see positives in everything we encounter in life. He maintained that everyone who walks into your life is either a friend or has come to teach you something. Let's take an everyday example.

You're driving to work and you're running late. As you go around a corner you find a car on your side of the road overtaking another vehicle, forcing you to slow down to avoid a head on collision with this imbecile. Incredibly, this cretin seems to apportion the blame for this near miss to you as he / she gesticulates wildly whilst mouthing obscenities at you as you pass each other.

This makes your blood boil as he / she obviously doesn't realise that you are an excellent driver who hasn't had an accident in years and you spend the next ten minutes revisiting the incident in your mind and getting even more worked up about it.
When you get to work you just have to tell your colleagues about the incident;

"I had a near miss with a lunatic this morning! I was coming around the corner at the High Street when this idiot attempted to overtake me and there was a lorry coming the other way…."

You then regale your colleagues with the full version, thereby once again increasing your blood pressure. None of this, of course, has the slightest impact upon the "lunatic" who is now far away causing chaos elsewhere and no doubt oblivious to the terrible harm he or she has dealt to you. No, instead it makes YOU feel worse as you delight in reliving the minute detail of your escapade with your listener, who may pretend to be listening but isn't really interested.

Now if instead of getting ratty when this person annoyed you with their driving, you had just shrugged your shoulders and thought "Ah well, no harm done." You would now be feeling a whole lot better.

You see, you think you feel bad because someone has done something terrible to you, but if you think that, you are only identifying with your ego or lower self. Your higher, spiritual, self is made from pure love and as such is incapable of feeling hurt. Instead of feeling aggrieved it simply accepts, says thank-you and moves on from the experience. The real reason you feel bad is because of your negative response to the offender.

In sending back curses or anger, you are out of alignment with your higher self and it feels bad. The only person it hurts is yourself.
So, the next time some idiot cuts you up on the road and then has the temerity to mouth obscenities at you, instead of responding in a similar fashion questioning their parentage, remind yourself that, as this person is clearly not a friend, he / she has come to teach you something.
It could be patience, restraint, forgiveness, or even some new expletives.
The amazing thing is, that if you don't respond negatively, you really do feel better.
"Happy Talk" means seeing all things as dreams, that is good rather than good or bad, happy rather than happy or sad.

If you can view life in this way, then you really do "have everything" as you have achieved spiritual mastery.

Esther and Jerry Hicks refer to a Rampage of Appreciation whereby they offer thanks for everything that comes along in their day, whether "good" or "bad". It's the same idea.
Nelson Mandela was able to view his long years in captivity as a blessing, rather than as a sentence.
The Dalai Lama has a similar positive view about the occupation of his homeland Tibet by the Chinese, recognising it as an exercise for him and his people in extreme forgiveness. If you can see the positive aspect in even the worst situation, then you will experience the dream, rather than the nightmare.

So, when all you have is dreams, then you have everything because, if you believe in your power to manifest anything in your life by your mind (including your dreams) then you really do have access to everything. I'll stop there. Look how much I've written about one line from one song.

Well, before I started writing, I thanked God / the Universe for manifesting a chapter for me, so it was relatively effortless on my part...I'm rowing my boat gently down the stream.

Do try this at home

What is your dream? It might be the ideal partner, a cottage in the country, a world cruise or your ideal career.
Whatever it is, start to really believe that it is achievable and make appropriate plans for when it appears.

Collect suitable cuttings from magazines and stick them into a "dream" scrapbook.
This will all help to bring your dream to you.

Be patient-with faith it will come in time, but you can't push the river! Instead, go with the flow.

5. Real songs written from the heart for the soul

Now that we've looked at how to create anything you want in your life with the power of your mind, let's consider the art of creation in a bit more detail to further empower you.

I'm going to use the example of writing songs as this is something I am well versed in, but the principles apply to any creative activity that you engage with.

We are at our happiest and most powerful when we are creating something.

I am a songwriter. I write songs.

Not just any songs mind, but what I call *"Real songs; Written from the Heart for the Soul."*

I will explain shortly what this means, but for now understand that to me music is much more than just nice little tunes with catchy hooks you can whistle or sing in the shower. It's about how you live your life, how you see the world, how you relate to others, what you believe in, the meaning of life and spirituality.

Not for nothing is music often called "the language of the angels." First of all, what are we doing or trying to do when we sit down to write a song? We are trying to express our feelings, our beliefs or our experiences through creating something. Man has had this urge for self-expression since the earliest times.

Have a look at the paintings by prehistoric man in the caves at Altamira in Spain which were created around 35,000 years ago. In those days you would think that their time would have been fully taken up with hunting, surviving and meeting the most basic needs of food and shelter.
And yet they found the time to create art for no obvious practical purpose.

They weren't aiming to see their work hung in a prestigious art gallery or to earn a good living by selling prints of their masterpieces to other cave-dwellers.

So why did they do it?

 It's because the act of creating something resonates deeply within the human soul and it always has.

It doesn't matter whether it's a painting, a song, a sculpture, a beautiful garden or a piece of crocheting - they are all creations.

As you have seen earlier in this book, we are all mini-creators, like God in miniature, creating our lives with every thought we have while awake. Creating is what we love to do because it's who we really are. In this way our basic desire to express ourselves has changed little since those earliest attempts at art.

We may have far more outlets for our expression these days than just a cave wall and we may be more skilled in producing our work, but the underlying motivation remains identical - self-expression.

For me "Real Songs" are those that inspire, motivate, move, elevate, teach, heal, encourage, empathise, comfort or energise the listener. They are not just about entertainment - they also lead the listener somewhere.

Examples for me would include "Imagine" by John Lennon, "Let it Be" by the Beatles, "The Sound of Silence" by Simon and Garfunkel, "Strange Fruit" performed by Billie Holiday and "Hallelujah" by Leonard Cohen.

These are "timeless" songs because they literally come from beyond time. Their writers tapped into the higher spiritual realms to produce timeless classics which relate to the human condition and, therefore, resonate at the deepest level with listeners, thereby making them popular and successful.

You will have your own favourites, of course, which may be very different to mine, but they will probably all contain universal truths which resonate so deeply with you.

There's nothing wrong with listening to songs purely for entertainment value, of course, and they have their place ("to everything there is a season"). When I hear Lennon ripping into the first line of "Twist and Shout" it never fails to send shivers down my spine, despite the fact that it is hardly a deep and meaningful lyric over a three-chord structure repeated over and over again ad infinitum.

There will always be a need for some fairly superficial songs for us men to embarrass our families by demonstrating our abilities at dad dancing at weddings. However, there comes a time in life when most people tire of the never-ending search for joy through superficial entertainment and instead start to look for something a bit deeper.

This usually happens in the fifties age group, although there are always exceptions. Some luminaries are early birds (like Lennon) and some are real latecomers. A couple of so-called world leaders spring to mind in the latter category, but best not go there...

I am also a John Lennon fan. If we study John's "Imagine" in a bit more detail, we will see why it is consistently voted the most popular song of the last 50 years. Despite being based on an almost childishly simple chord structure, played by Lennon who was himself the first to criticise his own rudimentary piano playing and with a minimum of additional ornamentation from other instruments, the song clearly hits home.

Musically, therefore, it is nothing to shout about.

There's no amazing solo, no vocal harmonies and a bare minimum of instrumentation.
The backing is simply there to support the vocal. Much of the song's appeal stems from the lyric.

It paints a picture of a utopian world where "there's no heaven" because the world is no longer separated from heaven as it is here on earth and all the people are "living for today", that is mindfully in the present moment, rather than longing for a better tomorrow that never comes.

He goes on to imagine a world where there are no false boundaries between people in the shape of countries and people are living their lives in peace in "a brotherhood of man".

Lennon is articulating a vision that most people would dearly love to see happen in the world. It's a genuine heartfelt plea and it touches people because we all know deep down inside that the current world isn't as it should be when we switch on the news (much better not to bother, by the way).
It doesn't matter that he even rhymed "one" with "one "in the chorus ("I'm not the only one/and the world will live as one").

The song's message is so strong it works anyway, despite the somewhat lazy rhyme that strictly speaking isn't even a rhyme.

The song's message is timeless - a yearning for world peace and Lennon is singing from the heart, as evidenced by his and Yoko's continued efforts to get the world leaders of the day to sign up to peace through a variety of bizarre publicity activities, for which he attracted a lot of criticism.

It didn't matter to him that he was subjected to ridicule because it got him publicity and he truly meant what he was saying and that's another reason why we warm to this song.

We can spot a liar straight away. "Bridge over troubled water" has a similar theme, but on a more personal level, bringing peace to the individual troubled soul. Incidentally, Paul Simon says he has no idea where the title of the song came from - it just appeared from nowhere.
More on this "divine inspiration" later.

"Real" songs then are about truth and that's why they are "written from the heart".

They are not made up little stories. They have no hidden agenda.

Their principal raison d'etre isn't to make money, but self-expression and a genuine desire to move the world forwards in terms of its spiritual growth.

When George Harrison released "My Sweet Lord" as a single he wasn't really thinking commercially, in fact he took a big risk and could easily have alienated his followers by including references to Hare Krishna in the lyric, which was quite controversial at the time and it could easily have backfired on him.

Of course, despite George's noble ambition to move the world forwards spiritually, he was also sued for plagiarism when it was ruled that his song was supposedly derived from "He's so fine" by The Chiffons.

The salient point is that "My sweet Lord" is now revered as a classic, while no-body remembers the other song. George also wrote from his heart and it still moves people, regardless of a dubiously subjective court judgment.

We are all bombarded with negative news on a daily basis, including so-called "fake news" (is there any other kind?) so, when someone releases a song embedded with real truth it really stands out from the crowd and literally demands our attention.

It is no coincidence (there are none in life, only synchronicities as we will discuss later) that, when people are asked to name their favourite songs, they are usually old songs.

There may well be an element of nostalgia in their choices, for sure, as certain songs remind them of key moments in their lives, such as when they got married, or when they met their partner etc, but that's not all. The truth is that there are very few songs out there nowadays being promoted by the media that have any real substance to them.

The music business and the entertainment industry as a whole has become so profit-focused that it has lost its interest in creativity.

So-called artists are hyped to the extreme for two years and then "let go". Rather than seeing artistic growth, such as the Beatles' extraordinary journey from 1963 to 1970, much of today's "product" is simply that - product. It may entertain some people for a brief period of time, but it has no deep and lasting meaning for them because it is so shallow, so there are few modern "classics".

So, we have truthful songs written with passion "for the soul".
Why for the soul?

Because the soul, or higher self, is truth personified. It vibrates sympathetically with truth, so it just loves songs of this type. The higher self is always trying to get you to see the truth, to ignore all the illusions of the world and see what is really out there, or in there, to be strictly accurate as the world is really a projection from your mind.

That's another topic for a future chapter.

The soul has one "sole" purpose in life, which is to lead you back to the truth and so it is delighted when you pick up on a truth in a song, or anywhere else for that matter, and as a reward and to show you that you are on the right track it makes you feel good.
That's why some songs really speak to us.

What exactly is this thing called the "higher self"?

Well, you have to understand that you are not just a physical being, but you are in fact multi-dimensional. The segment of you that is currently inhabiting a human body on earth is only a small part of the whole you which is simultaneously continuing to live other lives elsewhere.

You look in the mirror and you think that the face staring back at you is you, but it is only one part of you. Nevertheless, the human *you* is inextricably linked to the higher self at all times.

The higher self is the real you. It knows everything, it has all the answers and it is made of pure love.

The purpose of the human self is to experience all that it can so that the higher self can then know itself experientially. The higher self never interferes with what you are doing on earth, but it does offer guidance and clues to show you the best path available to you to learn what you came to learn.

When you follow those clues you are in alignment with the higher self and everything seems to go well, so you feel joy, peace or anything positive. You are rowing your boat gently downstream. If you choose to follow a different path you will find life is a long and winding road. The end destination remains the same, but the journey will be much more tiresome, including traffic cones and roadworks with long delays everywhere.

A useful image I use for this is that of the bumper cars or dodgems at a fun fair.
If you imagine that the car (and driver) are the human, physical self and the aerial at the back, which connects the car to the power grid above is the connection to the higher self.

As long as the bumper car stays in alignment or connected to the grid above then it has access to its power. If, however, it was to lose its way and crash off the track it would become disconnected from its power source and rendered pretty ineffective.

So, it is with the lower and higher self.

If you head off in a "wrong" direction you lose the power that is always available to you from above.

If you are in alignment with your higher self, things once again become relatively effortless, doors open for you and the "right" people magically appear in your life just when you need them. Just as there are other drivers on the bumper cars' track who are trying to crash into you and disrupt your journey, so too will life throw similar obstacles in your way as you journey through it.

But if you stay connected to your higher self, you will always come through.

That's what I mean by "Real songs written from the heart for the soul".

So how do you write one of these classics?

Well, it can't be easy, can it, otherwise everyone would be at it?

Actually, I would suggest it is easy.... *once you know how to do it*. Now let's be quite clear, I am not for one moment claiming that any of my songs are anywhere near as good as the classics mentioned earlier. I do know, though, that in my experience they resonate with certain people in the same way that the songs I class as classics resonate with me. And anyway, in a spiritual sense, success is not measured in terms of commercial success or popularity, nice though those are if they come along.

My approach is as follows but talk to other songwriters and you'll find a hundred alternative approaches. For me the music and lyrics are equally important and so I have to write both. The combination of music and lyric is crucial and I can't imagine trying to put someone else's lyric to my music or vice versa. They are completely inter-dependent.

I sit with my guitar, or sometimes the piano, and try to get out of my mind.
No there's no drugs involved, only tea!

I try to be fully in the present moment and empty my mind of all trivial matters such as how the Brexit negotiations are going (Ha! As if!). If I'm lucky, I will suddenly find I'm unconsciously playing something that sounds interesting and there's a spark of something there.

This doesn't always happen, of course. If it doesn't, I put the guitar down and try again later, maybe the next day. Eventually, something does come and that's the germ of an idea that now needs to come to full fruition.

A friend of mine, Nigel Somers, is an artist and he uses a similar technique when painting. He covers a canvas in a wash and then waits for inspiration to flower. He has no idea what he is going to paint. The resulting pictures resonate with me as deeply spiritual.

One of them is the cover art for this book and the band's first CD **"The Acoustic Rainbow".**

I then use the same process to try to move the song along a bit. Often at this stage I have little or no lyrics, but an idea of the chord sequence and the melody line and maybe an odd word or phrase that might lead to the final lyric.

This process may take hours or weeks - I just go with it. My song "I believe in Love" was written in twenty minutes! That is by no means the norm for me, but when it happens it is truly magical like the ancient art of alchemy which involves creating something wonderful from something base.

I was sat at the piano early one Sunday morning (about 6am which is a great time to write before your mind gets cluttered with daily dramas) and suddenly the whole of what became "Hold on" (a new song on our next CD), literally fell out of the sky and I had most of the song in an instant.
There is a story behind that song that is worth telling as it is directly related to what we are discussing here so bear with me...

I was at a very happy stage in my life as everything was going well with me, my family and friends and I had no reason whatsoever to write a song about holding on with your fingertips while life dishes out pain, grief and sorrow in your direction. Nevertheless, that's the lyric that appeared.

About three months later I received a shock telephone call from my brother telling me my sister, who was younger than me and a perfectly fit 46-year old, had contracted flu and had died very suddenly overnight.
This was devastating news, of course, and totally out of the blue. It took me some time to come to terms with it, particularly as she left behind three young children.

My wife suggested I try to write a song about it to help me to deal with the grief by channelling my energy into a cathartic song. I thought about it and realised I had already been given the song in readiness for what was coming – my song "Hold on";

When faith runs dry
As life goes by
If you're feeling all alone
And far away from home
When all is dark
Inside your heart
And colours start to fade
To silent clouds of grey
Hold on
Hold on

The song was subsequently played at my sister's funeral.

I know I was given the song in preparation for a forthcoming major event in my life to help me to deal with it. And because I've experienced the pain of losing someone close to me, I can empathise with others who go through the same experience (which is virtually everyone, of course, at some stage in their life).

So, this is a real song written (and performed) from the Heart for the Soul.

Of course, it's nice if it becomes commercially successful - I would be lying if I said otherwise, but really for me it's a success if only one other person gets something out of it and finds it a help.

I wrote a song called **"Feathers Fall"** and played it for the first time at a friend's meditational retreat.

A girl sat on the front row was in tears when I'd finished and assured me it wasn't my singing that had set her off, but the lyric in the song had moved her to tears as she could relate it directly to a recent event in her own life. It wouldn't matter to me if no-one else ever heard it or liked it because the fact that one person had found it soothing was enough for it to be worthwhile and, therefore, for me a success.

We all go through similar challenges in life at some point, and the chances are that a song will "speak" to others in just the same way, so it is unlikely to resonate only with a few people.

The human experience is universal and that's why music speaks so many different languages.

As I'm writing this, I am a volunteer on a book launch team for the actress **Roma Downey** who starred in the TV series **"Touched by an Angel"**.

She's not very well known here in England but is an A-list celebrity in America where she even has her own star on the Hollywood walk of fame. Wow.

Anyway, she has written a book titled **"A Box of Butterflies"** which is an account of her life story to date, filled with inspirational quotations from spiritual texts.

Roma writes with an almost child-like innocence and simplicity which I find really refreshing because there is no hidden agenda.

For me it's a "real book written from the heart for the soul" and as such it is bound to be a success. It isn't the greatest literary work ever written, just as my songs aren't the greatest songs ever composed, but the intention behind it / them is pure and that is what makes them so powerful.

When you try to improve the world in some way via your creations all of the powerful unseen energies of the universe come to your aid, just like "The Force" in "Star Wars"! The force is always with you but is especially powerful when you are in alignment with your higher self, as we discussed earlier with the bumper cars example.
Now you know how to access it, so use it in your own life and create miracles!
This is how many of the great works of art were created, be it paintings, sculpture, inventions or anything requiring creativity.

More often than not you will find the authors used a similar process of what I see as "channelling" from the higher dimensions to come up with their masterpiece.

This is where the traditional idea of an inspirational muse comes from. It is as if the authors are simply the mouthpiece for this universal energy to use.
Shakespeare was fully aware of this;

There are more things in heaven and earth, Horatio, than are dreamt of in your philosophy. (Hamlet)

Song writing is, as we have said, a creative process and when we create anything, we are accessing our inner power which is available to everyone, irrespective of their background, class, gender etc.

Jesus was at pains to choose ordinary men (and women, despite their lowly status in the four male-dominated Gospels) as his disciples to demonstrate that the power did not belong just to the ruling classes.

When Jesus said "Are ye not gods!?" to his disciples he was referring to our ability to create anything we put our minds to. Any human activity involving creation is powerful, whether it is painting, music, sculpture, crafts or knitting and we feel a pull towards whichever of these we are most interested in and good at.
We are on the planet to create.

That is our purpose and to experience life through our creations and the emotions they evoke. This is why we have so-called hobbies. In fact, most of us have life back to front as we spend most of our time doing a job we dislike and a tiny fraction of our existence pursuing our favourite activities in our spare time.
Happiness comes from reversing this.

I speak from experience. The next time you sit down to create something, why not try the method I have outlined above? Just go with the flow and don't try to force it. It doesn't matter what you are creating - you can use the same method as I do for writing songs…. or your own method if you find that works better for you.

The important thing is to create something. You will find it is always far more satisfying than just being a passive observer of life sitting in front of the television.

So what are you waiting for? Go and get started on your own masterpiece (after you've read the rest of this book, of course!).

Do try this at home
If you do not have one already, introduce a creative activity into your life.
It can be anything as long as you are producing something.
This will have great benefits for your health, happiness and peace of mind.
Try my method of creating by emptying your mind and just allowing yourself to be guided in whatever you are engaged in.

6. **How to be happy**

Let's tune into happiness now by looking at every day incidents that happen in all of our lives and how we can use them to our advantage. Look around you.

How many people do you know who are genuinely happy? I mean really happy, not just happy when it's the week-end or a bank holiday, or when they're on holiday or have just been paid or when the sun is shining.

Those are all temporary states of happiness that cannot last because they depend upon external events in time and space, all of which are only transitory and largely out of our control. It can't be Saturday every day and you can't be on holiday all the time.

How many of your friends spend much of their time grumbling about something or gossiping about someone?

It's easy to get into that sort of negative habit in a world where we are all encouraged to continually work harder in order to have more of everything so that we can achieve happiness by being seen to have more than somebody else. There is no end to this fiasco. It's a bit like the economic forecast for the country where each successive government is promising continual growth. It's not possible.

Every lesson that humans need to learn can be found exemplified in the natural world, where everything exists in perfect balance and equilibrium until man interferes. Nature does not expect continual growth. Plants flourish in the summer months, die back in the autumn, rest during the winter and begin to grow back come the spring to begin the cycle all over again.

They don't grow all through the year.

We are a part of nature, but we are currently living apart from nature.

This is not the way to happiness, it's the way to unhappiness which eventually leads to stress, burn out and eventually illness.

No wonder then that so many people today are simply not happy. We need to remember that every day is a new day and an opportunity to start your life anew.

The following is the start of a fairly typical day in the life of an ordinary person. It might be you…

The morning alarm goes off and you groan "Oh God! It can't be time to get up already!"

You crawl out of bed and peep through the bedroom curtains. "Damn! It's raining again!"

You turn the shower on and jump in before it's had a chance to run warm.
"Aaaargh! That's freezing! Damn!"

You put the kettle on and make some tea. Then you find there's no milk in the fridge.
"Did you forget to get some milk?" you accuse your partner, feeling increasingly irritable.
"I didn't forget! You were meant to get some!" is the curt reply you receive.
"I can't think of everything!" you reply feeling even more annoyed. You decide to make some toast for breakfast but find the bread you have is out of date and probably mouldy.
"Don't say we haven't got any bread either! What am I supposed to do for breakfast?"
"I told you I'm not buying bread any more. You know I'm on a diet!"
"You don't have to eat it! Just buy the damn stuff!"

You head off for work in a foul mood and nearly run the neighbour's cat over as you screech off far too quickly down the road. Somehow every set of traffic lights you come to is on red and you are following the slowest driver in the world who never seems to notice when they change to green, forcing you to honk your horn at him each time.

"Come on for God's sake!"

When you do finally pull up on the car park at work, you decide it's worth sharing your experience of following the slowest driver in the world with the world by posting it on Facebook or Twitter.
You get the idea. We've all been there, haven't we?

Let's take a closer look at what you managed to achieve in the first hour of your brand-new day.

You put out at least 7 negatives and zero positives.

You are looking at the world as a half empty glass rather than half full. By the end of the hour you are feeling annoyed, depressed and fed up.
What a great way to start the day! Of course, you are not doing anything "wrong", because you have free will and can choose to make yourself miserable if you want to. But if you continually put negative thoughts out into the world, that's exactly what you will get back.

Wouldn't you rather choose to be happy?

The first step to happiness is gratitude. Try to be grateful for what you have in your life. Instead of focusing on what you don't have, focus on all the good things you do have. In an age when, unbelievably, half of the world's population still doesn't have access to clean drinking water, you are more than likely to have much to be thankful for, not least that you are not one of them.
Let's revisit our domestic scene above but this time look for the positives that are there if we look for them.

The alarm goes off at 6.45am and you say a silent thank-you for being given another day on the planet to experience whatever it is you decide to create.

You get out of bed and peer through the bedroom curtains.
"It's raining. Ah well, never mind. I'm at work all day and it's just what the garden needs after that dry spell." you think to yourself.
You turn the shower on and jump in before it's had a chance to get warm.

"Brrrr!" you laugh to yourself as you jump out again, thankful that your partner didn't witness your actions, so it won't be shared with the world via social media.

You put the kettle on and make some tea. Then you find there's no milk in the fridge.
"Looks like we're out of milk. I'll just pop to the local shop to get some. Anything else we need?"

"Oh thanks! Sorry I completely forgot. Can you get some bread as well, please? I think that loaf has gone off".

"Okay. Won't be long."
You leave for work a few minutes later than planned due to your additional trip to the local store but feeling happy and content with the world.

Every set of traffic lights you encounter is somehow on green and you sail through them, arriving 5 minutes earlier than planned at work.

Okay so life isn't very often as black and white as these two examples, but the principle is the important thing here.

Every single little incident in life is an opportunity to express yourself in either a positive or a negative way. Don't ever forget that what you put out you always get back.

It's no coincidence that all the lights are against you when you are in a foul mood because you simply can't attract good things into your life if you are putting out so much negativity.

When you appreciate the world around you, life is on your side and things happen as if by magic because you are unleashing the awesome energy of the universe. And you will learn in a forthcoming chapter that every negative action or thought you have impacts far more widely than you would ever believe.

Everything affects everything else.

Your negativity is helping to slow the world's progress towards spiritual enlightenment – that's how powerful you are.

It's very easy to become annoyed at other people as in the examples above, but it is equally as easy not to. If you find you dislike a particular character trait within someone you meet or know, try to understand that they have come into your life for a reason - to reflect back to you an aspect of your own personality that you are not proud of.

They are like a mirror.

Their purpose in coming to you is to help you to see how your behaviour is impacting upon other people, so that you can then choose whether you wish to change your behaviour accordingly - they are actually doing you a service! If you keep sounding your horn at the slow driver in front, you will find lots of other slow drivers take his / her place when they turn off.

And they'll keep coming until you learn the lesson, then they will magically disappear.

We are however, only human and so there will be occasions when we do lose our temper and forget all the positive stuff. That's fine. Don't beat yourself up about it. We are not perfect and we are not meant to be.
If we were perfect, we wouldn't be here as we would have nothing to experience / learn.

The best thing to do when you lose it is to have your moment of anger and then let it go, rather than hanging on to it. Think of something that makes you smile and you will instantly stop the flow of negative energy. It could be anything like a holiday memory, your first baby, your pet dog etc. Anything that puts a smile on your face.

Try to understand that every time you think of yourself as a victim of something or someone, you are looking at life through the half-empty glass, rather than half full.

Nobody is a victim because, you will remember, you are the main cause of everything that happens to you in your life.

After a relatively short period of time, you will find that happiness becomes your normal state of mind and people will notice and want to be like you. Happiness is addictive.
Try smiling at people and see what you get back.

The other key ingredient to happiness is *what* you are doing with your life, as well as how you are doing it. Most people are conditioned to believe that they have to work, usually in a job that they don't want but think they need to pay the mortgage, bills etc. It is not easy to stay happy when you are spending most of your time doing something you dislike.

It doesn't have to be like this. Life is meant to be joyful, creative, vibrant and exciting, not dull and repetitive, unless the latter is something you have actively chosen to experience in your current lifetime, rather than thinking you have no choice but to accept the crummy job to meet your living expenses.

When I tell people about this, I ask them what they would really like to do for a living.

Their answers are usually something based on their hobbies, like cake-making, flower arranging, martial arts, writing, something with animals, sport and so on.

They don't *believe* they can make a living doing something they love to do, and so it doesn't happen. Remember that what you believe you create in your life. They have to believe it first and then they will see it. The truth is that you can be or do anything that you *put your mind to*- literally!

So take some small steps towards your ideal job or life. If it's possible, try reducing the time spent in your other job little by little while you build up your new career.

If you really enjoy what you do then you are doing what you came to do, and life will already be easy and joyful.
It's only difficult when you are doing something you didn't come to do.
So how do you find your true-life purpose?

Remember what I said earlier, it will involve doing something that you don't see as work, as a burden. It will be something you would do for free because you love it so much. Imagine yourself waking up on Monday morning so excited to get to work that you haven't slept!

That's when you know you are on the right path and you will begin to experience amazing synchronicities (you'll probably call them coincidences to begin with) which we will discuss in a later chapter. That's how I feel about song writing and about healing. You will have your own favourites.

The other aspect to happiness is mindfulness. This seems to be the latest fad judging by the number of adult colouring books now on sale in WHSmith's (other reputable newsagents are available).

Behind the hype, however, is a genuine aid to greater happiness.

Most people live their lives either regretting what they did or didn't do in the past and / or what they might / might not do in the future.

They spend very little time in the present moment.

Here are a few examples;

"I can't wait for my holidays- only 10 weeks to go!"
"If I get that promotion at work next week, I will be so happy!"
"Only two years to go to my retirement!"
"Why didn't I take that job I was offered five years ago? I'd have been a manager by now."
"I wish the Spring would hurry up! I hate the Winter!"
"Roll on the week-end! It's only Tuesday and I've had enough already!"

The problem with these thoughts is that the past and the future simply don't exist. There is only the eternal moment of now. And the more you focus on the past or the future the less you are actually living your life as you are only giving the present moment a cursory glance.
As a result, you cannot experience anything in depth, including happiness, which is what we are talking about.

You can never be completely happy if you are waiting for something to happen in the future or regretting what happened or didn't happen in the past.
To be completely happy you have to be in the present moment.

It's a bit like eating your meal quickly, if you are late for work, for example. You can't savour the different flavours and textures of the food you are eating for breakfast if you are gulping it down with one eye on the clock. You are using the food as a means to an end (fuel) rather than as a delightful activity in itself, stimulating the senses. Similarly, you can't experience complete happiness if you are not thoroughly immersed in the present moment and this is what mindfulness is all about.

So how do you get to be more mindful, more in the now?
The first step is you have to learn to empty your mind of the constant chatter going on...
"What shall I get for tea tonight?"

"I wonder how the kids got on at school today."
"I need to get that assignment written".
"I forgot to pick my suit up from the dry-cleaners".
"What's on the TV tonight?" And so on.
It's constant and at first, it's very difficult to switch it off.

That's why adult colouring books can be a useful tool. If you can immerse yourself in a relatively pleasurable, peaceful pastime your conscious mind will switch off to some extent, so you can then minimise the background chatter. It's worth a try.

Some people will find other pastimes have a similar effect upon them, like knitting. If you read any books on mindfulness you will find that they also try to teach you how to get fully involved in even the most menial of tasks in order to be in the present. Let's take doing the ironing as an example.

Instead of thinking "How many more shirts to go?" or "This is so boring." you should try to immerse yourself in the activity. Feel the different textures of the various items of clothing, feel the warmth from the iron, listen to the hiss of the steam, smell the aroma from the washing powder you used and so on. I have to confess that I find this almost impossible to do, but it is effective if you can manage it, so try it.
It might work for you!

Do try this at home

Begin to look at life with a half full glass mentality whenever possible. Notice how much happier this makes you feel. Contrast this with how you feel on those occasions when you forget and put out negativity.

There is literally a world of difference. Don't add to the world's negativity by sharing negative thoughts and experiences via social media.
Only share positive messages. If you can't say something nice, don't say anything.

7. There's no such thing as coincidence

So far, we have talked about creating the life you really want in order to find true happiness.

Now we are going to zoom in on how the universe gives you guidance all the time, so you will know for certain when you are on the right path, even when the physical world seems to be telling you the opposite by things seemingly going wrong.

When you're on the right path to carry out your chosen life purpose you will find little coincidences occurring all the time. They are messages from above confirming that you are on course and all is well.

You will have noticed if you've read this far that I have a thing about The Beatles and especially John Lennon. I truly believe that John is my chief spirit guide and he is never far away.

We all have spirit guides who assist us in our lives. Some come and go as we change our careers or progress along our life paths, others stay with us throughout our life. The chief guide is someone who takes a continual overview of our progress and sends other "specialists" to us when needed.

Some may be famous from their time on Earth and some not. In the higher planes the concepts of fame and celebrity are wholly irrelevant and meaningless.

There is no time or space where they are, so they can be in many places at the same time. John will, therefore, be a guide for many other people in the world, not just me. I still feel immensely privileged to have him "on my side" though.

How do you find out who your spirit guides are?

Simple. Ask him / her / them to make themselves known to you and then watch for the signs that will begin to appear.

Your chief guide is usually someone you have had a lifelong interest in, so you will probably say "Oh, of course!" when you find out who it is.
In this way it's never a real surprise, more like a confirmation.

In my case my music room was virtually a shrine to John long before I knew about his spiritual role in my life. Coincidence? I think not.

I just loved his song writing, his lyrics, his honesty and his desire to change the world.

How do I know for certain that he is my guide? Well, when I was doing my Reiki level 2 training with Bernie, we did a meditation exercise in which we asked our chief guide to visit us. In my mind I was sat on a bench in a field and John Lennon appeared, wearing his white suit, walking down the path that went past the bench.

He sat down next to me. I thought what do I say to John Lennon!?
"What do you think of my songs?" I blurted out.
"They're not as good as mine!" he replied!
I already knew he was my guide – I just *knew*. I could feel it, and your feelings never lie.

If you have a passion for writing, for example, it's likely that your chief guide will have been a successful author in a previous life. If you are a healer, you may have a medicine man from an Indian tribe and so on.

It doesn't really matter who your guides are, the important point is that, after they have passed over, they usually continue to have a keen interest in the same things they were passionate about whilst on the planet.

For this reason, they will offer whatever help they can to you to assist you on your life journey because they too want to see the world continually evolving.

They will have been doing this all your life, often without you realising, but you can speed your progress up immensely by actively being aware of their messages and following their guidance. Below are a few examples of things that have happened to me in this way to give you some idea as to what to look out for.

As you will see, some come directly from John and others are merely influenced by his presence. They are all very welcome.

Here's an example from a few years ago of my chief guide sending me a message via a friend.
I was sat in a coffee shop with my friends Steve and Benita, talking over spiritual matters. Benita is very psychic and she suddenly said to me;
"I've got a message for you from John!"
"Go on." I replied.
 "He says behold the new dawn!"
Just as she said it my phone pinged as a text arrived. I took it out of my pocket and started laughing.
"What is it?" Benita asked.

My friend **Dawn** had sent me a message which read "Thought you might like this." and attached was a photograph of John Lennon.
You couldn't write it.
I've had so many similar events that I can't begin to remember them all, so I've chosen a selection from those I can remember to share with you in this chapter.
Some are more impressive than others, but I've deliberately chosen a variety to show how you can sometimes find spiritual messages in the small things in your life, as well as the big events.

Here's another one featuring John.
I was visiting a client on a weekly basis to give healing in his home and I always set my portable couch up in the same corner of his lounge.

After a few visits I took a closer look at the picture that was on the wall right next to my couch. It was a familiar looking scene.
"Is that Central Park, New York?" I asked.

"Yes."

The picture is an evening Winter scene and features a bridge over a small lake, with the typical New York tall buildings in the background.

There are trees either side of the bridge whose branches seem to be pointing to a window in one of the buildings which has a bright light shining forth into the darkness. It's the Dakota building, which was home to John and Yoko and she still lives there.

As I said, he's never far away!

As I studied the picture, I felt him explaining its significance as follows. The bridge is a link between this world and the spiritual plane (where he is), but to cross it you don't go over the bridge, but through it.

The scene in the picture that you see looking through the arch of the bridge is much brighter than that of the foreground as there's much more light there. It's a symbol of how life is so much brighter "on the other side".

The other amazing coincidence in this picture is that the trees and the bridge just happen to form the shape of a giant swan!

The Swan was, of course, the pub in which my spiritual awakening began, as I've already explained in the first chapter.
As well as John, I also often feel George Harrison's presence nearby.

One day I was watching a repeat showing of the farewell concert for George on TV which was held a year after his death. I said a silent thank-you to him for the wonderful songs he wrote and for his spirituality which opened the way for many others to follow.

When I'd finished, I went outside to move my wife's car onto the drive as it was parked in the road. As I turned the ignition key the radio sprang to life and it was playing "Got my mind set on you." recorded by George. Just a coincidence you might say.

Next morning, I was moving her car back off the drive to get my own car out and as her radio came on, they were playing the very same song again. That was George just checking in. I understood that the title of the song was telling me that George was also helping me along my life journey.

These synchronicities are little signs that I am doing what I came to do, and I am not alone.

I was explaining to one of my clients that I had seen her as Julian of Norwich in a previous life while I was giving her a healing session.

This sometimes happens and I always take it that I am to tell the client what I've seen as it will help them, otherwise there would be little point in me knowing.

In case you don't know, Julian (!) was a mystic woman who wrote what is believed to be the first book written in English by a woman ("Revelations of Divine Love") in around 1395.

My client hadn't heard of Julian but took it on board, neither convinced nor sceptical. A couple of days later, she sent me a text telling me that she hadn't told anybody about Julian, but her sister had for some reason suddenly sent her a text about her. So she went out and bought Julian's book.

Here's another one.

I visualised a different female client as Akhenaten the Egyptian pharaoh and again I told her what I'd seen. It was only a few hours later that she sent me a message telling me she had gone back to work and a "rogue" email had somehow bypassed the organisation's security systems and found its way into the inbox on her computer.

It was an advertisement for an exhibition in nearby Telford of Egyptian artefacts from the reign of Akhenaten.

About two years ago the PA amplifier in my music studio packed up so I took it to my friend Steve's music shop in Lichfield to be repaired. He rang me a week later to say it was a right off unfortunately, as it was so old, they couldn't get the replacement parts needed.

I asked him to keep an eye out for anyone selling an old amplifier that I could buy as I didn't have much money.

A few days later he contacted me again to say a guy had brought just such an amplifier into the shop and asked Steve to sell it for him. I went over to the shop and Steve said take it home and try it before you buy. I did and it was perfect for what I needed so I went back to pay for it.

Steve wasn't sure how much the owner wanted so he said he would let me know when he next came into the shop as he hadn't left a phone number. I'm still waiting to pay as he hasn't been seen since. I have since found out that the amplifier did at some point in its past belong to Lichfield Cathedral, so I now see it as a gift from God, irrespective of whether I do finally have to pay for it or not.

I was in our local town centre a few years ago with my wife and son. As we were walking along, a man suddenly came up to me.

"Hey! You're Keith Forrest! I've got your CD! I love it!"

And with that he went on his way. The thing is, I had only produced a few CDs for close friends previously and this was before you could upload your songs onto the internet to be downloaded. Who was this guy and where did he get my CD from?

Oh, and by the way, how did he know who I was? My CDs have never had any photos of me on the covers and this was before the days of social media.
My wife and son were intrigued when I said I had no idea who he was. I told them it was a message from above saying that I was on the right track with my music and this incident would happen again

"legitimately" at some point in the future.

Recently I was wondering whether to share the truth about a friend's past life with her. I wasn't sure if she was ready or not. As I was sat in the lounge wondering what to do, I saw a van come down into our cul-de-sac. I recognised it as a van used by an all-female local garden maintenance company called "Garden Angels". I thought it strange they had come into our close as I look after virtually all of the gardens there and I had never seen one there before.

Sure enough, the van turned around and drove straight out again without stopping so I assumed angels were trying to tell me something.

A few minutes later my friend Moyra rang me for a chat and "happened" to mention a book she thought I would like called "**The Book of Deborah" by Maggy Whitehouse.**

So what? Well, the friend I was thinking of telling about her own past life is called Deborah…. I chose to tell her about her past life, and she took it completely on board.

Every day I choose an Angel card at random from a pack of 52.

They never fail to offer an insight into what I am going to be experiencing that day. Somehow the "right" card always gets chosen.

I shuffle the cards repeatedly until one falls out and that's the card for the day, so it is totally random (although nothing in life is random, of course. It all happens for a purpose.).
Last Easter I "chose" the same card for 5 days in a row - the ascension card.
What are the odds of that happening, choosing the same card five times in a row out of 52? It said to me that I was definitely on the right path and moving upwards!
I mentioned earlier that I have been helping on the book launch for Roma Downey's book "A Box of Butterflies".

When I was wondering whether to volunteer, the postman arrived and left a parcel outside our front door. It was something from the women's shop "Roman" that my wife had ordered. The item was in a bag that had been folded over and sellotaped so that instead of saying "Roman" it read "Roma".

Incidentally, I love the fact that "Roma" is "Amor" backwards - the Spanish word for love.

A few years ago, I was giving healing on a weekly basis to a guy who was recovering from cancer. He had married a beautiful woman from Thailand several years earlier and had written a book about her called "Thai Angel".

One morning I was standing outside our house talking to a neighbour when we both noticed a small ball rolling down the street towards us. It literally had appeared from nowhere as there was nobody else around. The ball stopped precisely where we were standing and I picked it up. It was transparent and had the name "Isobel" written inside it.

"Do you know any Isobel's?" I asked my neighbour.
Neither of us did and the road remained empty other than us two. I decided it must be a message for me of some sort whose meaning would reveal itself at the right time. That afternoon I went to do healing on my regular customer, and I mentioned the ball incident to him to see if it had any meaning for him.

"I only know of one Isabel and I haven't been in contact with her for years." he said, so we forgot about it.
The very next morning I got a phone call from him in a state of excitement.

"Oh my God! You'll never guess what's happened this morning!"
He went on to explain that he didn't have any copies of his book left as he had sold them all years earlier. He had decided a week or so earlier to see if he could find any copies for sale on the internet.

He had successfully located two second hand copies, paid for them on line and was awaiting their arrival in the post.

The morning after our discussion the first of the books had arrived in the post. When he looked inside the front cover, there was a handwritten message "To Isabel".

It turned out that the book had been given to her by the husband of the Isabel my client used to know and he was the publisher of the book. It had found its way back to its author.
And all this happened the day after a small ball came rolling down our road from nowhere bearing her name.

Here's a final example for you.

A good friend of mine recently opened up a garage selling old prestige cars such as old Jaguars, Morris Minors and so on. It's a lovely building and he had a spare room upstairs which he offered to me to use for healing. I gratefully accepted and brought a couch etc to the garage the following week, at the beginning of December.

I have been working under the name of **"Sparkle Reiki"** and had a suitable sign made for the door. When I got to the garage, I spotted that a new poster had appeared on the notice board of the pub that is directly opposite the garage.
It was a big colourful advertisement for Christmas meals, and it said, "Bring on the Sparkle this Christmas!"

Well, that was meant to be the final example, but I've just had another one!
Last week I went to visit a friend in hospital who suffered a major stroke about two months ago. She has improved tremendously since then, but still can't talk so finds it difficult to communicate.

I was talking to her about the food she was having, which was pureed due to her only just having relearned how to swallow. She obviously wasn't keen on the food so I joked that I would sort out some fish and chips for her next time which made her smile.

A few days later my wife went to visit her and it was tea time. You can probably guess what happened. They brought her a plate of fish and chips, so my wife helped her to eat it by feeding her. She wolfed it down.
My wife was really pleased that she had obviously made such great progress in the week since she previously saw her. When she'd finished eating, one of the nurses came to her bedside, looked at the empty plate and said, "She hasn't had this, has she?"

Yes, she'd been given the wrong tray. It was another patient's food. Well, I did promise her fish and chips and the universe delivered!

Similar synchronicities will surround you once you are following the correct path for your life purpose. You just have to be aware of them, open your eyes and stay alert. They are easily missed sometimes until you get used to them.

But don't go around actively looking for them as that doesn't work!

If you are consciously looking for a car with the number plate ANG E1 or similar they will not appear. Just be assured that they will come when the time is right. You have probably already experienced some but put them down to coincidence. There is no such thing. They are wonderful signs that show you all is well, no matter what is going on around you.

Another common sign that you are on the right path is finding a feather in unusual places.

As I'm writing this, one of my clients has just texted me to say she's found one in her bra!

They are a symbol of love from the angels and are often there to encourage you when things get tough, or to reassure you that all will be well, no matter what the world throws at you.

Shortly after my sister died, I was walking down a local road thinking about her when I suddenly felt tingles all over. I stopped and looked down. There on the ground was about 100 white feathers in a circle around me.

Feathers are used as signs primarily because we associate them with angel wings, but also with birds and flight. Birds have mastered the physical world because they are able to fly, and we humans are envious of their ability. In fact, believe it or not, birds are able to fly from one dimension into another.

Next time you have a clear blue sky on a summer's day, sit quietly outside and empty your mind. Look up at the sky and eventually if you are patient you will see birds suddenly appear from nowhere. They have flown into the third dimension from elsewhere and can do so with ease.

At first you will think your eyes have played a trick on you and they have come from behind a cloud or something, but they haven't. I've seen this over and over again. When you think about it, it shouldn't really come as a surprise that animals or birds have abilities way beyond ours.

We all accept that dogs' hearing range is infinitely greater than ours and they can hear things we aren't even remotely aware of because our sense of hearing is only calibrated to cover a much shorter scale. We also know that dolphins use a sophisticated radar system to keep track of where they are and what about the tracking system used by birds that fly thousands of miles to visit the same breeding site every year?

Guess what just happened?
I was just doing a bit of editing and was re-reading a later chapter which looks at songs about the human chakra system, including **"True Colours" by Cyndi Lauper.** I popped upstairs and my wife was playing that very song on her iPad. And no, she hasn't read any of this book yet.

Do try this at home

Keep your senses open to receive messages from your guides.

Every time something happens which you would normally see as a coincidence, take the time to consider it in a bit more detail to determine its true meaning for you and then act on it.

8. I'm loving angels instead

As well as having spirit guides, we also have angels helping us on our way.

They are always willing to help us, but we have to ask for their help. They cannot just intervene on our behalf as that would infringe our free will.

The world is in love with angels. They are everywhere. There are books galore about them, so I am not going to repeat what is already freely available out there.
Instead, in this chapter I'm going to give you a few examples of angel intervention in my own life to hopefully demonstrate their reality for you and what to look out for in your own life.

Often, angels take the appearance of humans when they interact with us so that we are not over-awed by their celestial appearance like the story of the shepherds at the nativity.

Here are a few examples…

This first is one of my favourite encounters with angels that happened shortly after my sister died.
My wife and I were staying in Banbury for the week-end, near to where my sister used to live so of course she was very much in my thoughts the whole time we were there. We parked up in the hotel car park and walked to the entrance door. There was a sign next to the entrance which proclaimed in big letters "GABRIEL WELCOMES YOU!"
Apparently, the manager's name was Gabriel, but I felt a by now familiar warm glow inside and knew the message had also come from above.

That evening we had tickets to see **Beverley Craven** in concert at the Mill in Banbury (my sister had interviewed Beverley a few years earlier so that was a nice connection).

We weren't sure how far the Mill was from the hotel, but we set off on foot with only 10 minutes to go before the start of the concert. As we were walking in what we thought was vaguely the right direction, we saw a man, woman and (presumably) daughter coming towards us.

My wife asked them how far it was to the Mill and could we get there in ten minutes? The man said "No, you'd better come with us and we'll drop you off." So, without a thought we all climbed into their car parked nearby and set off. We were sat in the back with the little girl and chatted with her.

"Have you got any brothers or sisters?" my wife asked her.

"Yes! I've got two brothers called Gabriel and Raphael!" she replied giggling.

As I'm sure you know, Archangel Gabriel is known as the messenger angel from the Bible and Archangel Raphael is the healing angel. I sat there in the car thinking I am being transported by a party of angels sent to help us by my sister.

We arrived at the Mill for the concert with perfect timing, of course. When we got back home, my wife was telling her father about our stay in Banbury.

"Which hotel did you stay in?" he asked.
"The Cromwell." she replied.
"Ah. Did you know that if you trace your family tree right back you are related to Oliver Cromwell himself!" her father announced.
Sometimes the synchronicities are just amazing.

Here's another example.

I was sitting having lunch at my mum and dad's one day when there was a noise at the front door. It was nothing like a normal knock. I can only describe it as sounding as if a giant bird's wing had brushed against the door, like a "whoosh!" We all looked at one another and I went to the door to see what it was. A young man was stood there,

beaming from ear to ear. He looked me straight in the face and said;
"Hello. I'm making people aware of poverty in the world."
Before I could say anything, my mum came to the door and
announced that, whatever he was selling, we didn't want any.

"Oh that's okay." he said. "I don't want anything. I'm just here raising
awareness."

With that he beamed another dazzling smile at me and said;
"Have a fantastic day!"
And he walked off.
"What was that all about?" my mum asked.
I wondered the same thing to myself and kept hearing the name
"Gabriel" resounding in my mind.

How many times have you had someone come to your door, not to
sell you anything, not to convert you to their way of thinking, not to
collect money for a good cause...but just to raise your awareness?

It was a first for me too. You make your own mind up as to who he
really was!

Here's an example from about 8 years ago, not long after my
awakening in Liverpool.

I had started to do some gardening for people and one day I was in
the front garden of one of my clients who had asked me to make a
gravel path for her. I was busy shovelling gravel with my head down
when I suddenly became aware of a man standing by me, smiling. He
was about 70 years old, tall and wearing a wide brimmed hat. He had
an air of powerful serenity about him.

"What are you doing?" he asked.
"Oh, I'm making a path." I replied.
"Yes you are." he said, smiling.
As I looked into his eyes I could feel immense power surging behind
them, totally out of place with his physical appearance.

"I'd like to give you this." he said, offering me a leaflet.
"Oh, I don't live here," I said, "but I'll pass it on to the lady who does".
"No. It's for you." he said and handed it to me. "Everything you need to know is in there."

With that he turned and walked off, but I could still sense immensely powerful energy surrounding me. The leaflet was all about the Bible.

Want another one?

I was playing in a covers band and we had a gig at a community centre which was linked to the Holy Trinity church next door. As soon as we arrived I felt that something important was going to happen. As we were setting our gear up a woman came over to say hello as she'd recognised me from when I used to work for the local council. As I looked at her I had a strong feeling I had known her a long time ago before this life.

"Don't I know you from a previous life?" she said, meaning, of course, my previous career in local government. I smiled to myself.

As we were sound-checking our equipment, the church next door was having its evening service and my amplifier suddenly started to act like a radio receiver so you could hear the minister's voice speaking through it. It had never done anything like that before at previous gigs.

"I see you have God speaking to you." joked our drummer, not realising how close to the truth that probably was. Many a true word spoken in jest.

After the gig was over, we packed the gear away and got into our cars to head home. It was about 1am and we were the only people left. I watched the others disappear off the car park and then got back out of my car.
I just knew I was not meant to leave yet because something significant was going to happen. I walked to the back of the church

building and waited in the darkness.

There was a beautiful white statue of Mary there, so I stood in front of it. It was very dark and completely silent. It was a clear night with no wind and lots of stars. Suddenly I saw a mist high in the sky which slowly formed itself into the shape of an angel. It started to descend in front of me until it got close to the ground and then evaporated away into nothingness. I got back into my car and drove home, knowing I'd been given a clear sign that I was following the right path and that angelic help was always nearby to assist me. I was, of course, ecstatic but decided against telling anyone about it at the time as I knew they would think I'd lost the plot again!

Angels are messengers from God and they use a variety of methods to get their message across. Sometimes they will form shapes in the clouds, send feathers, robins or butterflies that follow you around and sometimes they will talk to you through the voice of a friend.

Here's an example of the latter which I experienced shortly after my sister died.

Tracy had been doing some promotional work for the guy in charge of the Cornbury Music Festival who is called Hugh Phillimore. Hugh very kindly allowed me to perform at the festival after she had died as a tribute to her, which I was delighted to do. It was a lovely warm sunny day and I could feel Tracy's presence very strongly while I was performing.

A couple of weeks later, I was having a cup of coffee with my friend Steve, who had watched the show at Cornbury. We were just chatting about ordinary stuff, when he suddenly turned to me and said;

"You know when you played at Cornbury the other week...?"
"Yes?" (we hadn't been talking about Cornbury)
"Well, your sister was sat on your shoulder while you were singing."
"Oh, er, thanks."

And with that he returned to whatever it was we had been discussing beforehand. I knew it wasn't him speaking. Steve is a person who calls a spade a spade and this just wasn't his kind of masculine language. He seemed disconnected from what he was saying too, as if his voice was being used by someone else to get a message to me, which was indeed the case.

I left it for a quite a while before I asked him if he remembered saying these things. He looked at me as if to say "What?" He had no memory of it whatsoever. The message for me had come through him, not from him and they had chosen to use words which not only sent me comfort but also made it very clear to me that it was not Steve speaking. If, for example, he had simply said "Your sister was there." it simply wouldn't have had the same impact.

Sometimes I have received gifts from angels as I go about my work of offering healing to people.

If someone is terminally ill, I never charge for the healing because it just doesn't feel right to do so. Sometimes I have to drive quite a distance to visit such clients in their homes and on several occasions, I have come back to my car afterwards and found that the amount of fuel in my car has mysteriously increased since I drove there. It's a locking petrol cap, so either it's a divine gift or some kind person is breaking open my petrol cap just to donate some petrol to me, and then somehow locking it back up again with no sign of damage.

How else do you explain it?

One time my gauge was on empty when I went to do a healing and it was a third full when I came back. I always say thank-you. Remember - what you give out you will always get back tenfold.

If you want to know more about the angelic realm, I recommend any of Lorna Byrne's books such as *"Angels in my hair"*.

Do try this at home

Look out for angelic intervention in your own life.

Ask for help from them when you need it and be open to suggestions from them in response to your request.

They may come in pictures, symbols, feelings or any of the ways shown in this chapter.

Remember – you have to ask!

9. John, Paul, George and Jesus

This chapter is all about how popular culture is also used by divinity to spread the message.
We do not receive divine guidance just from our spirit guides or angels.

Just as Jesus used parables from everyday life to get his message across to the ordinary people, so too is the popular culture of today used in a similar way. We'll start by looking at the biggest band ever. The Beatles split up nearly 50 years ago, but their music still fills the airwaves. They are still held in reverence all these years later.

Why is this?

You may think there can't possibly be much left to write about The Beatles. Every song has been analysed over and over again. Well, one of the (many) reasons I think they are still worshipped is because many of their best lyrics are still revealing themselves, still producing shocks and surprises, despite having been studied for decades by Beatles enthusiasts and even academics.

You want an example, so let's take a fresh look at "Hey Jude".

Yes, I know you've heard it a thousand times, but bear with me. Most people know the story of how this song was written by Paul McCartney on his way to visit John Lennon's first wife, Cynthia, following her break-up with John who had recently left her for Yoko Ono.

Paul was feeling sorry for John and Cynthia's son, Julian, and the effect the split would have on him, so he started to form an idea for a song to cheer him up while driving to their house – "Hey Jules, don't make it bad, take a sad song and make it better".

By the time the song was finished, "Jules" had somehow morphed into "Jude" and the song seemingly took on a life of its own.

At a time when relations between John and Paul were somewhat strained, John liked it because he thought it was about him and Yoko with Paul seemingly giving his approval to John's new relationship ("Remember to let her into your heart, then you can start to make it better."), while Paul thought he was singing about Julian. So, whose meaning was the right one?

Well, you could argue that the writer (in this case Paul) ought to know what he's writing about, so surely his version is the most accurate? I would disagree.

Paul's interpretation is of course entirely valid, especially for him, but it doesn't mean it's the only meaning. I believe that often artists think they know what they are writing about or creating, but some years later come to realise that they weren't really writing about what they thought they were and there is a far deeper meaning behind their creation. I have certainly found this to be the case with some of my own lyrics.

Are we saying that Lennon's interpretation is the "real" one then? Well, no. That was just how the song resonated with him in a very personal way, especially with regard to his relationship with Yoko. He was probably looking for confirmation that he was doing the right thing leaving his wife and son and so found his own meaning in Paul's lyric.

For me, there is a much more profound take on the lyric to this song. Paul may not even be fully aware yet of what he wrote, or to be more accurate, channelled. For me the most successful lyrics are literally given to us from higher realms when we are "in the zone".

Paul also famously channelled "Yesterday" whilst asleep, waking up with the entire melody in his head and thinking he was humming somebody else's existing song.

With "Hey Jude" this is one of those lyrics where I believe divine inspiration also definitely came into play. So, here we go with my personal take on it...

Assume the word "Jude" is short for "Judas".
Assume that the narrator is God.

Suddenly the lyric takes on a whole new theme - one of forgiveness.

Not just any old forgiveness mind, next to Adolf Hitler, Judas Iscariot is probably the most hated man in history, rightly or wrongly (let's not get into a debate on that, or we will never finish this book).

Let's assume for our purposes that the Bible story in which he supposedly betrayed Jesus with a kiss on the cheek, handing him over to the Romans to be crucified, is accurate, as the majority of Christians believe. Far from being condemned for his actions, in the lyric Judas is being told by God to "take a sad song and make it better" by remembering to "let her into your heart".

For me "her" refers to the feminine aspects of divinity - compassion, forgiveness and nurturing, for example. In other words, this is God himself / herself / itself telling Judas "Cheer up! It's all right really.

Forgive yourself for what you have done, and things will look a whole lot better."
In the second verse God tells Judas "don't be afraid" and "You were made to go out and get her".
To me this is saying Judas was following his life path. He was carrying out what he was created for.
You were meant to have this experience, so stop beating yourself up about it. Not only were you meant to give Jesus up to the Church authorities and Pontius Pilate, but you even volunteered to do it before you incarnated.

Time and again Jesus says that the saviour must be handed over, beaten, abused and put to death just as the scriptures prophesised and without Judas this aspect of the divine plan wouldn't have happened. As the saying goes, "To err is human, to forgive is divine."

This song lyric resonates with us because it contains a divine aspect of truth, that no-one is a lost soul, no matter what mischief we (or Judas) may get up to.
That's good news.

Even if we are not consciously aware of this interpretation (and I've never heard of it being described this way by anyone else previously), it still hits the target in our subconscious which is hardwired to the eternal truths. Have you ever wondered why you like a particular song or piece of music?

Try to analyse it and it's quite difficult to pin down. It's not just about the great guitar hook or the clever lyrics. In many cases it is because there are deeper aspects to the song which trigger deeper emotions within us, and it doesn't get much deeper than extreme forgiveness.

To err is human, but to forgive is divine. Little wonder then that "Hey Jude" is consistently voted one of the Beatles' most popular songs.

Whether you agree with my personal interpretation or not is unimportant. This is what it says to me when I hear it. Maybe you have your own equally valid and individual interpretation. The best pieces of art offer multiple interpretations as to their meaning and they are all correct.

How could anyone offer a definitive explanation of what a painting by Picasso is meant to say?
As I said at the beginning, The Beatles are still producing surprises and even the most well-known of their songs can still be interpreted in new ways.

Let's now turn to "Strawberry Fields Forever" to see what alternative meanings might be lurking inside Lennon's masterpiece.

Again, most commentators tell the story of a young Lennon climbing over the fence into the grounds of the local Salvation Army building called Strawberry Fields and how he uses that image as a way to explore his childhood memories, just as Paul does with "Penny Lane".

For me, though, this Lennon lyric is far more than that.

Strawberry Fields is described as a place where "nothing is real" so there's "nothing to get hung about". Lennon is detailing how he is seeing the three-dimensional world around him where there really is nothing to get uptight about because none of it is real anyway. It's all an illusion as we've discussed earlier like the magic show.

He goes on to describe how most people live their lives "with eyes closed" and "misunderstanding all you see". He sees himself as different from the crowd ("No-one I think is in my tree.") because no-one else seems to see through the illusion of 3D existence, but he also expresses some doubts about his own sanity ("Always, no, sometimes think it's me.") before affirming that "I know when it's a dream".

To me Lennon is describing the spiritual breakthrough he was experiencing at the time and, understandably, struggling to put into words concepts that are beyond the confines of three-dimensional reality on Earth.

"Let me take you down" is an invitation to "follow me!" He is showing how the world is not as it appears and once you can see through the veils of illusion you too will realise that "It doesn't matter much to me." He doesn't have all the answers and his vision is clouded because it is at least partly fuelled by the psychedelic drugs he was using at the time, but nevertheless he is seeing glimpses of the truth. He went on to explore this theme again in his solo work in songs such as "Mind Games".

Amazingly, the first signs of his spiritual awakening are to be found on the very first Beatles LP "Please Please Me" in the song "There's a Place".
In it he describes a place where he can go when he feels low and that place is his mind where there's "no time".

Compare this to the lyrics of most "moon and June" pop songs of the day and you can see how special The Beatles were, even in the early days.
So why exactly were they so special and what is their story really all about?

Well, as with most things of any substance, it works on several levels. In the physical world theirs is a traditional "rags to riches" tale of the underdogs being buffeted by the storms of life, refusing to give in and ultimately succeeding against all the odds and sticking two fingers up at the establishment, which had turned them down repeatedly and ended up fawning all over them like lap-dogs.

Despite being turned down by the most influential people in the music business, they became the biggest band in the world ever. This story resonates with us because it shows that anything is possible, just like a Dickens novel. It takes us back to the chapter on dreams.

The Beatles had a collective dream and they realised it through grit, determination, talent and a series of amazing "coincidences" that brought all the right people to them at just the right time. But that's not all…if we move beyond the physical world it is clear that The Beatles were carrying out a spiritual task assigned to them before they incarnated.

Yes that even includes Ringo! He was the most popular Beatle in America. Without him they would not have been as popular there and that was very important in the overall plan bearing in mind that country's standing as a world power.

Of course, like many before and after them, they succumbed to the lure of fame, wealth and all its trappings along the earthly path, but they soon realised that success did not bring them the peace and joy they thought it would.

That's why they embarked on their own spiritual journey with the Maharishi in the late 1960s and later on both George and John in particular continued their quest for personal enlightenment in their own individual ways.

The Beatles' story is fascinating because the way the right people (Brian Epstein, George Martin, even Ringo) showed up at just the right time is a clear indication that they were being guided from above.

There are no coincidences in life - nothing is random. Instead, there are synchronicities and they occur with increasing frequency the closer you are to your life purpose.

This is what the saying "I did it on purpose." really means. When you are "on purpose" things just flow naturally.

So what was the Beatles' spiritual purpose?

I would suggest several. They moved the world forwards. They helped to break down class barriers. In the 1960s the UK was split into very clear divisions of class and a rich / poor divide.

The Beatles showed that anybody from any background could "make it". It even became cool to have a regional accent. They opened up creativity by writing their own songs as nobody else did that at the time and they made popular music an art form with their ground-breaking album "Sergeant Pepper" and subsequent releases.

They were leaders in the hippy movement, helping to spread the love and peace message, which again changed everything and shook the Establishment to the core.

They played a significant part in preparing the world to climb up several rungs on the ascension ladder. George helped to break down barriers between Eastern and Western religions and John went on post-Beatles to work for world peace in his own inimitable style.

Not bad for four scruffs from Liverpool!

So, we can find traces of divine messages in the Beatles' songs, but they can also be found all over the place in other artists' songs and indeed other forms of entertainment.

Here's just a few examples of some songs with spiritual overtones;

"Spirits in the Material World" – The Police (this is exactly what we are – spirits having a human experience, rather than the other way around)

"After the Deluge" – Jackson Browne (a salutary tale for mankind about the fall of Atlantis)

"The Dark Side of the Moon" – Pink Floyd (a whole album about what's really going on in the world...and beyond)

"I believe I can fly" – Lighthouse Family (believing is seeing)

"Solsbury Hill"- Peter Gabriel (his spiritual awakening, like Lennon's "Strawberry Fields Forever")

"Starman" - David Bowie

"Starman" is a particularly interesting example. It tells the story of an extra-terrestrial who has "parked" his spaceship just outside Earth and is pondering whether to come and introduce himself to humanity.

He's not certain whether that would be a good idea because it might be too much for people to take on board and might blow their minds.

We are indeed currently being helped by more advanced races or "beings" from other planets at this critical time in the planet's history. **Neale Donald Walsch** explains what is happening on the planet in his latest book, **"Conversations with God Book Four- Awaken the Species"**.

David Bowie was writing about this forty-five years ago, helping to prepare us for the future that is now today. In fact, the whole album "Ziggy Stardust and the Spiders from Mars" can be viewed as a spiritual piece of work.

Ziggy is a fictional Messiah from Mars who happens to play guitar and sing. His words resonate with the fans who follow him around, worship him and demand more and more from him until eventually he is destroyed by the very planet he has come to rescue.

Sound familiar? Yes, it's a space-age alternative take on the Jesus story, who was also very different to everyone else, drew large crowds to him and who was eventually crucified by the very people he had come to inspire.

Bowie's fictional story became reality when his fans started to see him as Ziggy, rather than David Bowie and began to almost worship him with their obsessive adoration. David himself started to believe he was Ziggy and decided to end it before he went too far by retiring the character in 1973 at the very height of Ziggy's popularity.

Even in songs that aren't particularly weighty we can find little references to spirituality.

Again, the writers or the artists themselves may sometimes not be aware of these "clues", but that doesn't mean they're not there and are valid.
Here's a few examples of songs relating to the human chakra system for instance (which also features on the iconic "Dark Side of the Moon" cover) ...

"True Colours" by Cyndi Lauper

"Firework" by Katy Perry

"She's a Rainbow" by The Rolling Stones

I'm pretty certain Mick and Keith didn't sit down to write a spiritual song about the divine energy flowing through the human body.

Nevertheless, the reference is there - as popular artists of the day they were used to channel divine messages from the higher planes so that more people would "tune in" to the message.

This is the higher purpose of popular music and indeed popular culture itself. It's making advanced spiritual concepts more readily accessible for ordinary people (just like Jesus used the language of his day in parables), even if only through the subconscious.

Here are a few more.

"Hotel California" by The Eagles (a song about the soul being stuck in the 3D world and desperate to ascend to the higher planes. Same theme as "I want to break free" by Queen and "Somewhere over the Rainbow")

"Viva la Vida!" by Coldplay (a song about reincarnation. Chris Martin sings about being a King in one previous life and in another a road sweeper.)

"Angels" by Robbie Williams (about the divine help available to us at all times which will never forsake us)

"Heaven is a place on Earth" by Belinda Carlisle (this is exactly what we're working towards)

You get the idea.

When you start to look around you will find many others and the Beatles helped to start this all off.

You may have noticed, however, that there are far fewer influential bands around nowadays than in the 1960s and 70s. This is because worshipping rock gods has run its course. It's a modern-day equivalent of the idols and gods ancient civilisations worshipped. Instead of looking to others to provide inspiration, the next task facing humanity is for each person to find the answers within themselves.

We are all "rock gods"!

Hero worship does not lead anywhere – it is a dead end.

Music will continue to evolve to provide spiritual inspiration, rather than traditional rock and pop star values.

The Beatles' influence will continue to resonate.

The Beatles were indeed far more than just a pop group...

Do try this at home

Listen to your favourite artists' songs with fresh ears and look for similar messages to those I've highlighted in this chapter.

Once you open your mind to this you will discover that songs are literally teeming with similar references to help to show us the way.

Have a look at the lyrics to "Show me the Way" by Peter Frampton.

Lots more references there!

10. How does Frequency Sound? 440 versus 432Hz

This chapter builds on the previous one by showing you that it is not just the lyrics of popular songs that often contain spiritual signposts.

Even the very fabric of music can be used for similar purposes, as you will see.

If you are at all interested in music and are of a certain age like me, you will no doubt have debated the relative merits of listening to music recorded digitally (such as CDs or downloads) versus old-fashioned vinyl.

There is no doubt that digital recording offers amazing clarity which is difficult to match with vinyl, but despite this vinyl remains popular and has in recent years become increasingly so.

In fact, in 2016 vinyl regained its position as more popular than CDs in England, selling £2.5m compared to £2.1m digital.

Why is this?

Those who prefer vinyl often claim that digital recordings lack the warmth that vinyl possesses. If you look at the science behind this claim it is actually very valid. Digital recordings do not capture the full sound wave, due to the way they "sample" and then copy the sound they are recording. Vinyl works in a different way. The disc has a groove carved into it that matches up exactly with the shape of the sound wave, so it records everything.

This produces a richer texture of sound which you can actually hear if you compare the two methods.

A preference for vinyl can't just be dismissed as a nostalgic yearning for the past, it has a genuine scientific basis.

I have mentioned this to demonstrate that we need to keep an open mind when considering alternative viewpoints that might otherwise be seen as subjective nonsense.

But let's move on.

You may have heard about another ongoing debate related to how music should be recorded. This one is about tuning and there's plenty of stuff of varying quality about it on the internet. As with all these things, I will offer my perspective, but leave you to make up your own mind.

We are not going to get into heavy science here, as I failed my Physics "O" Level (Ouch! That shows my age.) so here's my simple guide to tuning.

Music recorded at 440Hz means that the middle A (the one above middle C on the piano) is tuned to give its note at a frequency of 440hz.

One Hertz (1Hz) equates to one cycle per second. This tuning has become the industry standard so most of the music you hear on the radio, in your car, via your iPhone etc is recorded at 440Hz. Before this standard was agreed upon, different classical composers used different tunings as to their individual preferences.

Some early classical music may still be in an alternative tuning when you listen to it. So far so good.

So, what's with this 432Hz?

Well, there is a growing view that this slight variation is more in sympathy with the human body's natural rhythms and, therefore, it makes the listener more comfortable / peaceful / joyful with the listening experience if the music is tuned down ever so slightly to 432Hz.

You will find ardent supporters of this theory on the internet and others who are equally convinced it is a load of new age rubbish. Who's right?

Well, first I'm reminded of a quote usually attributed to the German philosopher Arthur Schopenhauer who said;

"Truth passes through three stages: First it is ridiculed. Second, it is violently opposed. Third, it is accepted as self-evident."

It is certainly true that, throughout human history, many of the greatest discoveries went through this painful three-stage birthing process. So just because something challenges our preconceived ideas of what's normal, doesn't mean we shouldn't sit up and give it a fair hearing (literally in this case).

As a healer and Reiki master, I am well used to being at best ignored by some members of the medical profession, despite the amazing results I have witnessed with healing which defies traditional Western knowledge of the human body and its capabilities for self-healing.

In the not too distant future, I have no doubt that Western medical practice will encompass healing alongside its more traditional approach. It will have to if the NHS is to survive. Over-prescription of drugs such as antibiotics has led to a point where illnesses are becoming resistant to them. Something has to change.

There is also a view held by **David Icke** (love him or loathe him) and others that anything ridiculed by the Establishment is most definitely worthy of your attention because why else would they spend time and money in doing so, other than to dissuade you from learning the truth?

It's a valid argument. So, let's keep an open mind.

To test out this theory, we recorded one of our songs at both 440 and 432Hz and then played both versions to a few friends without telling them the difference.

When asked which they preferred, they all chose the 432 version!

When asked why, the comments were "It draws you in more." or "It feels better." Now you will probably find other examples on the internet where similar experiments have been carried out and it is claimed that people chose the 440Hz version, or that they were equally divided.

What can we make of this?

Well, let's assume that they are all telling the truth, to begin with. My view is that so much depends on the listener, who they are and where they are on their own spiritual journey.

It's well known that witnesses to a vehicle accident often give widely differing accounts of what they saw, some claiming it was a man in a white van and others a woman driving a blue lorry.

In a similar way, different people respond in different ways to the healing that I offer. Some feel heat, some feel cold, others see colours, some see or feel very little and some say they left their body and were looking down at themselves lying on the couch.

They are all telling *their* truth and are responding in individual ways to the same stimulus of healing energy.

Now, even modern-day science accepts that everything is made of energy and as such can be manipulated and influenced. With the healing process we have healing energy acting upon human being energy and we obtain a wide variety of results as shown above.

The healing energy never varies as it is a constant from the divine source. I conclude from this that different people respond in entirely different ways to exactly the same energy.

To come back to the issue in hand, music is energy and again so are we.
For those people who are further down the spiritual path than others, the music recorded at 432Hz may well be resonating more deeply

with them for reasons not yet understood by science. Perhaps it is similar to the phenomenon called sympathetic resonance whereby an un-plucked string on a musical instrument vibrates in tandem with a plucked string with a harmonic likeness on another instrument in the same room.

Conversely, people who have not progressed as far spiritually may feel absolutely no difference between the two versions or may even find 440Hz more appealing as it is more familiar to them.

This is my personal view. Both are "right" and neither is "wrong ".

It is vitally important to understand that being further down the spiritual path does not mean that person is somehow "better" or superior than someone else. That would be spiritual snobbery and the world has more than enough of that already thanks to religion. No, we are all on the same path and progressing at our own speed as it really isn't a race.

You can take as long as you like (and as many lives as you wish) to reach enlightenment. Inevitably, because of my own interest, many (but not all) of my friends are into spiritual matters and so find music recorded at 432Hz more appealing.

If you find it difficult to take on board that there are possible undiscovered merits in listening to music recorded at 432Hz, consider the following.

If you are middle-aged, think back to your childhood.

If someone had told you then that later in your life we would all have mobile phones that are mini computers with digital cameras connecting you to something called the internet from which we could glean the answer to virtually any question, play any piece of music, contact virtually anybody anywhere in the world in less than a second, would you have believed them?

If you are younger, would you have believed we would have an intelligent personal assistant such as Amazon's Alexa or Google Home (no doubt other brand devices are or will be available), which will happily turn your lights on and off or change their colour or play you instantly any song you ask it to?

Technology is moving so quickly that we can barely keep up with it. Surely it would be extremely arrogant and very short-sighted to think we now know it all and there is nothing out there waiting to be found?

If someone had told you back in the 1990s that in your lifetime vinyl records would overtake CDs in sales would you have believed them? Always keep an open mind.

Whether it's recorded at 440Hz or 432Hz, music is powerful and different types of music affect us in many different ways. You may be aware, for example, that supermarkets often use laid-back background music to encourage you to linger longer and not rush round the aisles with your trolley.

That's not because they have a genuine interest in your health and safety, but because that way you are likely to spend more, of course. The thump, thump, thump of the repetitive bass drum in dance music is designed to induce a mind-numbing trance-like state for dancers. Dance and trance have been closely linked for centuries, of course. Just look at the dances of North American Indian tribes preparing for battle, for example.

Heavy rock songs are used by corporations such as the WWE (World Wrestling Entertainment) to whip the crowd into a frenzy so that they enjoy the show (and don't take too much notice of how fake it all is. Hmm. Just like the "real "world?).
The Acoustic Rainbow songs are intended to give the listener healing as well as normal listening enjoyment.

How?

First, we used a minimum of electronic sounds, preferring instead to focus on natural organic sounds wherever possible.

The drum kit is a Cajon kit, with a wooden bass drum and snare.

The acoustic guitar features on all of the tracks, the electric guitar only sparsely.

Band member Nigel's sax and clarinet are real instruments, as opposed to virtual.

The overall result is a reasonably genuine organic sound, far removed from much of today's synthesised pop.

I sometimes think of it as being the opposite to Phil Spector's "wall of sound" approach. Don't get me wrong - Spector made some fantastic records that I really admire...but they don't resonate deeply with me on a personal level because there's so much going on. I admire his work, but I'm not personally moved by it the way I am by the simplicity of "Imagine".

Lots of people love the sound of Nigel's sax. Others really like the acoustic guitar's tone. Somehow, these more "natural" instruments strike more of a chord / resonate with people when compared with electronic instruments. I think it's to do with the way the notes are created.

Nigel has to blow hard and form his mouth into a certain shape to produce a note from the sax. Each note is subtly different as inevitably he can't keep blowing at the same velocity, neither would he want to as it would sound boring and he would quickly expire.

It's the same with the guitar as each note plucked or strummed is an individual subject to variables such as strength of attack on the string, different types of vibrato and so on.

Somehow the electric piano or other electronic sounds we use just don't get the same response from the audience. It's nothing to do with playing ability. It's the way the electronic sounds are produced without much interaction from the instrumentalist.

Essentially, a note on an electronic keyboard is produced by pushing a key which makes an electrical contact via a switch. Anybody can flick that switch to produce the note, whereas it takes lots of practice to produce even a single reasonable note on the saxophone.

Our bodies pick up on these subtle differences and resonate with them.
It's for this reason, in my opinion, that the human voice is the most popular musical instrument ever.

It is capable of the most subtle variations from a whisper to a scream and because it is produced from inside another human's body, it is almost as if we are getting a glimpse into that person's soul.

The words the voice is singing are equally important, of course. The lyrics in our songs are carefully constructed to gently guide the listener along the spiritual path, without preaching. Words are sacred and very powerful ("In the beginning was the word and the word was with God and the word was God.")

Every song has ideas in it to bring the listener more peace, more joy and more happiness, some of which we are analysing in this book. We recommend listening with headphones on and eyes closed for maximum benefit, allowing the healing to wash over you.

People often say that our music makes them feel peaceful, content and relaxed, which are the three words they also use the most often to describe a healing session with me.

One of the reasons for this similarity is the intention behind the two activities, or what I call the power of intent. When I am carrying out healing on a client, I am holding the intention to give healing in accordance with his / her highest good.

There is no other agenda.

I am simply sending healing energy / love to them. It's not my energy. It is freely available for anyone from the divine source. I am merely a channel to pass it on to people in need. Because of its pure intention, that energy is very powerful.
Love is the most powerful energy in the universe.

Similarly, the intention behind The Acoustic Rainbow's songs is to offer healing / positivity / love to the listener and, therefore, it is also powerful. That doesn't mean everyone will like it - some won't. That's fine. If we all liked the same things, life would be very tedious.

Even the band's name was carefully chosen to reflect some of the ideas being presented here. Incidentally, none of them are new ideas as they've been around for centuries in various guises, such as The Mystery Schools' and The Ageless Wisdom's teachings and are scattered throughout the world's religions, albeit often distorted to fit particular agendas.

So, what does The Acoustic Rainbow signify?

Here is what I was thinking. Human beings are literally a living rainbow as we have 7 main energy centres in our bodies called chakras which are well known to holistic therapists. There are many excellent books and articles written about the location and function of each chakra, so I do not intend to go into unnecessary detail here. Suffice to say that they each have their own colour which mirror the 7 colours of the rainbow;

1. *Base chakra – red*
2. *Sacral Chakra – Orange*
3. *Solar Plexus Chakra - Yellow*
4. *Heart Chakra – Green*
5. *Throat Chakra – Blue*
6. *Third eye Chakra – Indigo*
7. *Crown Chakra – Violet*

The lower three chakras (Base- Solar Plexus) are linked to our physical existence on earth.

The upper three (Throat-Crown) relate to our spiritual existence.

The Heart chakra provides a balance point or fulcrum between the two groups.

So the rainbow in our name is really the living rainbow, the human being, encompassing all aspects of our existence, both physical and spiritual.

Why an Acoustic Rainbow?

Well, first I like the idea of putting two words together that you don't usually see paired as it helps the name to stand out. Also, there's a nice correlation with music as each chakra resonates with a note in the musical scale and this can be used as the basis for sound healing. The main idea, though, is that we are attempting to present the full spectrum of the human experience through organic, natural non-electronic sounds, especially the human voice.

In short, I think of The Acoustic Rainbow as the human voice.

Needless to say, we released our album recorded at 432Hz. I took the view that most people wouldn't be bothered whether it was 432 or 440 and those who would be interested would prefer 432 for the reasons given above. Win-Win!

Do try this at home

Why not search out some music recorded at 432HZ and see if you feel any different listening to it.

11. A healthy mind in a healthy body

This is the last chapter in which we are going to look at you as an individual on the planet, before moving on to consider world-wide issues and beyond.

They are in reality one and the same, but more on that later.

What's the first thing you ask when you meet someone you know? "How are you?"

Health is the number one preoccupation of most people who've left their youth far behind, with the weather a close second. This is largely the result of the conditioning we have received since the day we were born as we will consider shortly.

Our never-ending quest for more money, a bigger house, a new car and more "things" disappears instantly the minute our physical presence on the planet is suddenly threatened by an unexpected and potentially fatal illness.

We all want to be healthy and to see another birthday. It's such a critical subject for many people and, as you will see, despite some fantastic progress in some areas, in many ways the Western medical world still has so much more to learn.

Health and healing are such big subjects that one chapter in this book can only skim the surface. Nevertheless, I've tried to pick out some of the most important things to help you to understand where health and illness really come from and that the age old saying that is the title to this chapter is really what it is all about.

The standard Western approach to solving an illness is to firstly diagnose what is physically wrong with the patient's body and then to correct the fault by administering drugs or medicine.

As an example, Doctors routinely prescribe anti-depressants for people suffering from depression, anxiety and so on. Whilst these may sometimes be useful as a short-term support aid, they rarely provide a long-term solution because they focus on the person's *symptoms*, rather than the root of the problem.

Long term use can, of course, also lead to addiction and a host of other physical and emotional problems. There isn't a single tablet or pill without undesirable side-effects because they all upset the body's natural chemical balance.

This standard approach to healing is flawed firstly because it is essentially *passive* on the part of the patient. He / she is simply told to take this medication in accordance with certain instructions governing dosage and regularity and then all will hopefully be well. It's as if the healing process has absolutely nothing to do with the patient.

This can never be wholly effective because any healing is being done to the patient,
rather than by the patient.

Western medicine also generally treats the body as a collection of parts that can be treated in isolation when one of those parts breaks down.

The body is really far more than a collection of parts. All those parts are inter-connected and work as a collective. If one organ isn't functioning properly the whole body will be affected in some way and, most importantly, the cause is unlikely to rest within that particular organ.

In truth, as we've already discussed you are far more than just a body.

You are a multi-dimensional being. All of those aspects of you are interrelated and they all impact upon each other. Any illness you are experiencing may have its root cause in all sorts of different locations. Physical health is intrinsically linked to spiritual health, hence the title of this chapter.

This is why treating the patient holistically is so important.

Every physical ailment can be traced back to an emotional imbalance, in other words the real problem is located in the mind, which then generates symptoms in the body to "warn" you that something in your life needs to change.

These days it is often stress that triggers the physical symptoms, such as headaches, migraines or upset stomachs. A friend of mine has been receiving hospital treatment for various different problems in different parts of the body over the last few years. Each problem is being treated separately by different consultants with little thought to the others and no contact between them.

Not surprisingly, the progress being made is painfully slow as the consultants are individually treating three symptoms of a deeper problem, which can only really be sorted out permanently by a holistic approach.

See how all of this fits together with our earlier discussions?
The mind is all powerful. It's behind everything, including illness.

When you consider the conditioning that the mind goes through every day (as also discussed earlier), it is hardly any wonder that it sometimes succumbs to the bombardment of negative imagery all around us and generates illness in the physical body as a way of saying "Give me a break! I've had enough!"

Every other advert on the TV is for a cold or cough remedy during the Winter months, alongside numerous reminders for the absolutely essential flu vaccination. We are told from our earliest days that as we grow older our bodies will of course begin to wear out, just like a machine.
We may need a new hip, we can expect some arthritis in our joints and we will definitely need glasses by the time we hit middle age.

Of course, as we largely *believe* what we're told, we subsequently create these outcomes for ourselves with our minds and the cycle continues because it's been "proven" to be accurate.

Here's an example of this - men's prostate trouble.

By middle age most men are getting up several times in the night supposedly to empty their bladder, although some actually struggle to pass urine once they are up. The widespread belief is that this is perfectly normal for men of a certain age so we should expect it to happen to us. That's why it is so prevalent.

I am most definitely in the age group that this is normal for....and I never get up in the night, so I must be abnormal. Why don't I get up? Because I don't believe I need to so I (literally) never give it a thought.

Without thought, the mind doesn't get involved and so the problem isn't created.

Now before we go any further, I want to emphasise that my health is not the product of luck, genetics, fanatical exercise, rigorous diet, super powers(!) or any other such idea, as I will demonstrate. The main difference between me and other people who are not as "lucky" with their health as I am is simply the level of belief we hold about our self-healing abilities.

I have complete faith in my body's ability to look after and to heal itself, should the need arise.

That's the only key difference.

Colds and flu are another good example. I haven't suffered from either for as far back as I can remember- probably since I became a healer- and no I don't have the flu vaccination.

I don't expect to get a cold and so I don't get one, even if I associate with people coughing and sneezing all around me.

Occasionally I might feel a few symptoms beginning to appear such as the odd sneeze or a slight tickle in the throat. All I do is think "Thank-you for sending even more health and well-being to me today." and by the next morning it has always disappeared.

Trust me - you can do the same if you believe it! Believing is seeing! One more example then, my eyesight. I don't wear glasses because I don't believe my eyes will ever wear out. Why should they? My body is not a machine. Every cell in the human body is continually regenerating, so there's really no need for anything to wear out with age.
Things *do* wear out in people because the conditioned mind believes they will, and the body always obeys the mind.

When I go to the opticians for my check-up my eyes are invariably the same as they were two years ago at the previous check-up. By the way, in case you were wondering, both my parents wear glasses, as does my younger brother so it's no use you trying to play the family history card against me.

When I last went to the optician's, our society's conditioning was brought home to me when the young optician (in her thirties?) asked me the following, prior to examining my eyes;

"Do you wear glasses for distance viewing?"
"No, I don't need to." I replied.
"Oh, okay, just for reading then?"
"No."
"No? Oh, so when did you last have your eyes checked?"
"Two years ago and they were fine."
"Hmmm."
Her assumption was obviously that, because of my age (58 at the time), I would surely need glasses. The subsequent examination proved that I didn't need them.

The optician noted me down as "abnormal".

I had another recent experience, this time with a nurse at the GP's surgery. I don't usually visit the doctor as I am never ill, so don't need to, but on this occasion, I received an invitation from the surgery to have my vital functions checked at a "well man" clinic.

At first I thought I wouldn't bother for all the obvious reasons, but then I decided maybe my male ego was being a bit arrogant in refusing, so I relented and went.

Two weeks later I went back to see the nurse for the results. Everything seemed fine - blood pressure, kidneys, liver, cholesterol etc. She told me I was very healthy for my age. Then she asked if there was any family history of heart problems in my family and I replied yes, on my mother's side.

She typed that into her computer then turned towards me;
"In view of your age and your family history, you should consider taking a statin."

"I'm sorry?" I said. "You've just told me how healthy I am. Why would I want to take anything when I'm healthy?"

"Government guidelines would recommend you consider taking one." She replied.

I pointed out that she hadn't asked if the family history involved over-weight relatives who drank and smoked. "We don't take those factors into consideration." she said.

I left the surgery with the Government leaflet about statins, which I immediately donated for recycling in the first rubbish bin I came to. I wondered how many other people had visited surgeries and been told the same and had started to take unnecessary medication on that basis.

Needless to say, I am not taking a statin, or any other medication, and I do not intend to start.

So far, I am happy to report, that against all the odds I have somehow survived to the advanced age of 60 and feel healthier than ever. You don't have to believe me, of course, but this is how I maintain my health and you could do the same. It's your call.

I am going to shift our attention to more serious illnesses now.

I've never been in hospital as I've never been seriously ill, but I've met lots of people who are in my work as a healer.

A client of mine was terminally ill with cancer throughout his body, which had also been ravaged by the effects of chemotherapy. Two weeks before he died, I was sat talking with him and he came out with the following profound statement;

"I've come to the conclusion that everybody probably gets cancer two or three times in their life, but they don't know about it, and so their body just deals with it and gets rid of it.
It is when you are diagnosed with cancer by the consultant that you go into decline and are in trouble."

His words, not mine, but I believe from my own experience there is much truth in what he said.

Of course, the consultants are doing their utmost to cure patients, and many are no doubt deeply upset when they lose patients, but generally this continual focus on illness isn't helping. They have been trained in the Western approach to medicine. They focus on the cancer and the shortened life expectancy of the patient and the (awful) side-effects of the limited options for treatment they have available to them to offer.

Health and well-being just do not get a look in.

Consider the following quote from **Eckhart Tolle in his book "Practising the Power of Now";**
"The belief in a label that someone attaches to your condition keeps

the condition in place, empowers it, and makes a seemingly solid reality out of a temporary imbalance. It gives it not only reality and solidity, but also continuity in time that it did not have before."

In other words what he is saying is that the medical diagnosis is actually prolonging the illness!

Once the patient has been told he / she has cancer and there is an X% chance of survival and the only chance is chemotherapy and the likely side-effects are hair loss, nausea, sickness and so on, he / she takes all this negativity on board and helps to unconsciously create these outcomes.

I see examples of this all the time when I have clients come to me for healing.

Some have invested their belief in chemotherapy, some have refused it. If they truly believe the chemo will cure them, then usually they go into remission. Sadly, in many cases, their cancer returns a year or two later.

Why is this?

Well, it's very difficult to have complete faith in a cure when the consultant administering the treatment tells you the percentage of likely success and / or of its returning.

In fact, no-one in the medical profession is going to guarantee a complete cure because they don't believe it themselves as they have seen some people respond to their treatment and others not and the likely prognosis they offer is built on what they have experienced with their previous patients.

They certainly wouldn't want to offer "false hope" (there's no such thing, by the way). So, after a period of time of elation because the patient is temporarily given the all clear, his / her conscious mind starts to think "I hope the cancer doesn't come back." or "I wonder if

I'm in the 20% who will see another 5 years." or "I wonder if that pain in my side is the cancer returning." and if you keep thinking something it will eventually manifest in your life, as we have discussed earlier in this book.

That applies even if it's something you don't want to manifest, like cancer. What you focus on, you get more of.

I see this so many times with my own clients.

Someone will come to me with an ailment, maybe a bad back for example. When they come back for a second visit, a week later, I ask them how they've got on since I saw them. More often than not, the conversation goes something like this;

"I woke up the morning after I saw you and felt great. My back pain was almost non-existent."
"What about the day after?" I ask.
"Still felt great."
"And..?"
"I was fine till a few days had gone by then I noticed the pain creeping back to normal."
"How is it today?"
"Funnily enough, it seems to have gone off again today."

I explain that this is all perfectly normal. The conscious mind doesn't like to be proved wrong. It created a bad back for you and it isn't about to let you get rid of it that easily without a fight.

It waits for an opportunity to sneak back in with thoughts such as "I can't just expect it to go after one treatment. I've had it for years, after all." or "I've got to expect some aches and pains at my age." And the more of these thoughts you have, the more energy you are giving to the reappearance of your ailment.

In most cases, the client is pain-free for longer after the second treatment and then the third and so on.

There is no normal number of sessions appropriate for everybody for a permanent cure, but as a general guide I suggest most people try about 6 weekly sessions with me before deciding whether they are "healed" or not.

The reason why the pain often dissipates the day they are coming back is because they are already subconsciously anticipating the positive outcome of the next treatment.

My friend Steve rang me a couple of weeks ago asking if he could come for some healing for his bad back which he'd had for some time.

I arranged for him to come the following week and, in the meantime, sent him a first draft of this book for his comments. When he came for the healing, he told me how he'd felt that recently he had lost his way a bit and just reading the draft had put him back onto the correct path and, you guessed it, his bad back had disappeared on its own.

The focus of the individual's mind is not the only factor affecting health, of course. Diet and exercise have their part to play (see below), but it is the key ingredient in whether a person recovers from illness or not, irrespective of the type of treatment administered.

This is why two patients with the same cancers, given the same drugs can have totally different outcomes. One may recover fully and the other pass away. The first is likely to have had a much greater belief in the drugs than the second. The level of belief will have been influenced by a range of factors including the prognosis given by the consultant, any family history of a similar illness, the person's own susceptibility to worrying and so on.

This is also why placebos can work. You can give an ill person a pill containing nothing but sugar and tell them it is a guaranteed cure and the patient often recovers.

It's their belief in the treatment that brings about the cure, not the treatment itself.

It is vitally important, therefore, for the medical practitioner to take great care in what he / she says to the patient as this will have a direct impact upon the patient's belief and ultimately their chances of survival.

For many cancer patients their lives become an endless round of drugs and side-effects and it is very difficult for them to focus on positivity (and so maximise their chances of recovery) when they are feeling so poorly.

Two of my clients have recently experienced the following, and I swear that these are genuine.

Client A was told by his oncologist "You do know that the cancer will come back, don't you?"

It hasn't by the way, because he has a strong belief in the healing he has experienced.

Client B, who was having chemotherapy, walked into her consultant's room and the first thing he told her was "You look pale." How many people being pumped full of poison look like they've just come back from a holiday abroad? He then went on to say, "You need to get your affairs in order at home."

If other patients had been given these comments, who do not have belief and / or knowledge of what the body can do to heal itself, then their future progress would have been seriously affected.

Words are powerful, especially from people in positions of authority.

I do not intend to criticise Doctors and Consultants because they have their patient's best interests at heart…. but it is time more of them broadened their thinking to encompass other approaches, alongside their existing treatments. Healing and other therapies are complementary to traditional medicine, not a replacement.

Here are two examples of clients of mine who have defied all the odds medically speaking.

Phil was an old acquaintance of mine who suffered a seriously debilitating illness in 2013.

He had Miliary Tuberculosis, Meningitis, a spinal stroke which resulted in paralysis, liver and kidney failure, bowel haemorrhage and Hydrocephalus. Following conventional medical treatment, he was not expected to survive and, if he did, the prognosis was that he would have a very poor quality of life with little mental capacity.

He did survive against all the odds but when I met him again following his illness he was confined to bed at home, unable to move his left leg at all and had limited cognitive abilities. He began to have a weekly healing session with me.

Fast forward to today and he is firing on all cylinders mentally and walking with a frame, whilst he continues to improve physically. He has even been able to go back to his old job. Phil is the only person known to have survived all this in England.

Polly came to me with a brain tumour. She had been given only months to live by her consultant, unless she agreed to chemo or radiotherapy, which she had refused. She came for a weekly healing session for about 6 weeks before going back to hospital for a scan.

The scan showed that the tumour had drastically reduced in size and was no longer life threatening.

Today she is fully back to normal and the tumour has gone. The only treatment she received was healing.
Both clients demonstrate the power of belief. They refused to listen to the conventional medical opinions and had faith in what we could achieve together.

It doesn't get any better than that!

12. Is it all just about belief?

Do diet and exercise play any part? Yes, they do.

It is sensible to eat a balanced diet and to exercise regularly. Just as important, though, is your belief system about diet and exercise. If you believe they are good for you, then they will be. Of course, most people would think they are good for you because they are conditioned into that way of thinking. We all buy into that premise, so it really is a good idea to eat healthily and to exercise to supplement whatever belief you have about your body's abilities to self-heal.

As an example, I've been a vegetarian for thirty odd years, I don't drink or smoke and I go to the gym on average twice a week.

Here are a few more thoughts on the subject of healing.

First, take a moment to appreciate the amazing body that you have at your disposal. Understand that it is always looking out for you.

If you are experiencing pain, it isn't because your body is letting you down somehow or trying to spoil your fun, it's because the pain is trying to tell you something about your health. It's often said that people who suffer a minor stroke have had a "warning" that a change of lifestyle is required to safeguard their future health.

That is 100% correct.

Your body is saying "Look, I've put up with this abuse for a while now, but I have your best interests at heart and I'm telling you we need to see a change if I'm going to be able to continue to support you in your life purpose!"

People often reach for the pain killers to alleviate their suffering.

Numbing the pain may provide a necessary temporary relief, but it doesn't help long term unless you make the required change of lifestyle, whether that is to quit smoking, cut down on alcohol, change your diet or reduce your stress. Blocking the pain out with medication doesn't mean the problem has gone away, only the symptoms. If you continually numb the pain with pain killers the body will eventually raise the bar and offer you another chance to change before it's too late.

The pain is trying to tell you that something is wrong and just blocking it out with pain killers will never solve the problem.

Just a word of caution about medicines and tablets.

It is, of course, wholly inappropriate to suddenly stop taking any medication you have been prescribed by your doctor, irrespective of my comments about their value and side-effects.

A gradual withdrawal from medication over a period of time as directed by your GP is the only way to come off them. This gives the body time to adjust its chemical balance itself.

The body will always try to get rid of something that it really doesn't find beneficial to your well-being. So, if you go out and drink ten pints of lager the chances are you will be ill soon afterwards as the body does its best to get rid of the stuff before it can do any damage to your liver. It knows what's good for it and what isn't.

That's why chemotherapy makes people ill.

It destroys both good and bad cells in the body and damages the immune system so the body does its best to regurgitate the toxins before they do the damage.

In "Conversations with God" Neale Donald Walsch recounts how God explains to him that the human body was designed never to wear out.

It only appears to wear out because we believe it will. Conversely, the body can and will heal itself if left to its own devices.

Most people don't leave it to sort itself out and instead introduce other ingredients, all of which complicate the situation further and very often prevent or at least hinder the body's recovery.

If the body can heal itself, why do we need to come to healers like yourself I hear you asking me. Good question. You don't.
But you don't believe you can do it all yourself, so you do need to come, at least for the time being.
In the future most illnesses will be dealt with by the person allowing their body to self-heal, rather than through coming for treatment from a practitioner. That is some way off though, so in the meantime there is a very definite need for healers, not least to help to educate the public at large about their own healing abilities.

In truth, when I offer healing to a client, I am simply reminding their body that it can heal itself. It's not my energy that is really doing the healing but theirs.
If you decide you want to try some Reiki healing, or any other alternative therapy, how do you choose the right healer for you?
The answer goes back to an earlier chapter- trust your feelings.

No matter whether a healer has been recommended to you, charges a lot or a little for a healing session, or has great feedback on their Facebook page, go with the person who feels right for you. Healing is, sadly, no different to every other human activity.

There are some fantastic healers who have devoted their lives to the art of healing, there are some who do a good job generally, others who dabble a bit "on the side" and some who are not in the business for any of the right reasons.
All of human life is here, as with any profession.

If you go with your feelings, you will be drawn to the right person for you. For the best outcome, try to avoid feeling like you are fighting the illness you are facing and instead see it as yet another experience that will eventually pass, no matter how challenging the present moment is.

As a healer, the hardest thing to learn to accept is that offering healing to a sick client doesn't always lead to a cure. People sometimes explain an early death by saying "It was just his time to go" and there is truth in that statement.
Once the soul has completed what it came to do it will leave the planet as it has no reason to stay.

Of course, from our limited three-dimensional view of life it very often appears that the person hasn't completed everything, leaving behind young children for example. This can be difficult to accept,-but we simply do not know what the soul chose to experience and so we struggle to understand why anyone would choose to leave their life "early".

Sometimes healing means offering the client help to deal with whatever he / she is facing, to come to terms with their situation and to try to accept it.

One of the most gratifying experiences I have had relates to two young patients from different families who came to me for healing. They weren't cured of their conditions, which were already extremely serious when I first met them, but I gave them as much help as I could before they passed away. Some people might say that I "failed", but I know for sure that the healing really helped them both and the proof is that both of their mothers have since come for healing for themselves.
There are no words...

Do try this at home

If you are suffering from an existing illness, whether it is a common cold or a serious medical condition, change the way you think about it when it comes into your mind.
Turn it into a positive such as "Thank-you for sending me health and vitality today." irrespective of how you are feeling. It will make a real difference and will eventually become your natural response.
Always think health, not illness.

13. The three railway tracks

So now we are moving on to look at world-wide issues and how they affect you as an individual, alongside how you can and already do impact upon them.

Remember that we are living inside a magic show where nothing is real – it just *looks* real.

In truth the entire universe is just a hologram, a projection from your mind. What happens if you slice a hologram in half? You get two halves, both of which contain the whole holographic image.
Not only that, if you take a tiny piece of the hologram and separate it from the whole it will still contain the whole holographic picture, rather than just a small part of it.

As we are living inside such a hologram, it therefore follows that everything in it is just a smaller version of the whole, including us.
We are indeed all one. Hold on to that thought for now...

The railway track is an image I use when explaining to clients about the nature of reality on Planet Earth and what's really going on.
I want you to picture three railway tracks, but instead of being side by side, they are instead situated one above the other.

The middle one looks like a normal silver rail track on the ground that we are all used to seeing. It looks a bit rusty and well worn. In parallel with that, but about 20 feet below in the ground is an identical track which mirrors exactly the bends and straights of the upper one, but this one has black rails.

A third track also follows the exact pattern of the lower two, but it is way up in the sky, beyond the sight of the human eye. Nevertheless, it is very real, in fact it is the only real one out of the three and, therefore, the only one that really matters.

It is shimmering gold in its ethereal appearance.

All three tracks are connected invisibly, so whatever happens on track one also happens upon the other two levels, both above and below, although the outcome may appear to be quite different. Got the image? Okay, so we have three rail tracks stacked one above the other.

What do they signify?

The middle one is physical life here on the planet in the 3D world we call Earth. It's what you see when you look out of your window. It's the big news stories you read in the press and watch on the TV. It's also all the little dramas that men and women get lost in every single day of their lives.

Let's turn to the second track, the one below ground so it's hidden from human sight. This is what is happening covertly behind the scenes of the first track. You might watch a politician speaking and on the level of the middle track you take his / her promise to do this or that at face value.

At the level of the second (darker) track lies the hidden agenda that the politician is really working to but doesn't want you to know. This is very often the opposite of what he / she claims to be working towards.
Everything that happens on the first track also occurs on the second track, but with a different aim.

The third track is easily the most important. Let's call it "the divine plan".
This level is what is really going on in the world and beyond.

It is at this level of understanding that everything happening at the lower two levels is neither good nor bad, it just *is* and it is all working towards the same goal, that is the spiritual ascension of the planet, regardless of what we or anybody else think is happening at those lower levels.
Even though the politician may be saying one thing (track one) but

meaning the opposite (track two) it doesn't matter- both are "right" in the divine context (track three) and moving the planet forwards despite seemingly conflicting agendas between tracks one and two. How clever is that? Well, what do you expect from God!?

This third level of understanding is how spiritual masters see the world.

Everything happens for a reason and nothing is good or bad - it just is. It isn't easy to attain this level of insight and maintain it when everything in your life seems to be going wrong. Nevertheless, it is the (only) way to lasting peace, joy and happiness. In some ways the three tracks mirror our own structure of body, mind and spirit in ascending order.

Let's take a concrete example of how this might work in practice, rather than just theory.

I'm going to focus on something that most people (including me) in the UK feel passionate about - the National Health Service. Let's examine what's happening at the 3 levels.

At the physical level (the middle track) the media is filled with "horror" stories about the failings of the Health Service. Missed targets, long waiting times, failing Trusts, wrong prescriptions handed out, botched operations, rogue consultants and, of course, increasingly inadequate funding leading to a national shortage of doctors and nurses, putting patients at severe risk.

No matter how many times politicians say how much extra money or staff they have brought in since their election, the harsh reality is that things seem to be getting worse, despite the sterling work dedicated NHS staff are doing which goes way beyond what they are paid to do.

It's a pretty grim picture on this track with rust creeping over the railway track as it fails to deliver, and the NHS is in danger of falling into disrepair like a disused railway siding.

What's going on behind the scenes underground on track two?

Well, let's just say for argument's sake that the people behind the scenes pulling the strings don't see the NHS as a priority. They see it as a drain on resources and would prefer to do away with it altogether and move completely to private healthcare.

Of course, to announce that would be political suicide for any Government, so instead they reduce the funding continually until it fails, and they can then bring in the private sector cavalry, at a suitably inflated price of course.

I don't want to focus on this level too much as this book is all about positivity, but at face value things look pretty grim for the future of the NHS on the second track, which is why it's coloured black.
At the third level, the only one that really matters, things are naturally going to plan!

How can I say that, bearing in mind the funding difficulties outlined above? I will explain.

First of all, let's be clear that the NHS is full of dedicated, hardworking professionals for whom I have the utmost respect. There are some amazing people in the Health Service.
My wife is one of them.

They all work far too many hours, many unpaid and they are totally dedicated to their profession.
As you will see in the penultimate chapter to this book, I owe my grand-daughter's life to the skill and care of the health professionals working in the NHS, so I have absolutely no intention to criticise.

Despite their dedication however, most people would agree that the NHS is failing. It is, but not in the way the Government likes to point out with its missed targets and performance indicators.
They are meaningless nonsense, often designed to be unattainable.
It's the easiest thing in the world to set an impossible target, knowing

that the organisation has no chance of attaining it, thereby "proving" that it's failing and provoking a public outcry.

They can then use the public's demand for something to be done as an excuse for bringing in the private sector to "put things right". This is not a new trick. It's been around at least since Roman times and probably much longer!

The real reason the NHS is "failing" is because it is often focused on the wrong thing - illness.

As you know, what you focus on you get more of courtesy of the "photocopier" universe.

Health (or illness) is of course no exception to this rule. As discussed in the preceding chapter, the more you think about illness and label it as so and so syndrome, the more you are giving it energy and are attracting it to you.

Western medical practice is underpinned by diagnosing what's wrong with the patient and then administering the "right" medicine to correct the supposed imbalance in the patient's health.

If you visit the hospital the consultant will do his / her best to tell you what's wrong with you, what they will do to put it right and the likely side-effects of any medicines they prescribe.

If you are suffering from a potentially terminal illness, you will probably also be told what your chances of survival are likely to be or how long you've got left.

Most people understandably believe what they are told by a suitably qualified health professional and so the diagnosis subsequently proves to be pretty accurate because they then create the very outcome they've been told to expect.

That way it is reaffirmed and will be used again the next time a patient with the same symptoms comes along, because it's "proved" to be reasonably accurate.

In truth, it is accurate mainly because the patient believed what he / she was told and therefore made it happen. It's a self-perpetuating cycle. This is how a family history of illness is created.

If we look at other approaches to healing, for example from the East, we will see that the Western approach has serious shortcomings. It takes virtually no account of the body's amazing abilities to self-heal, as described earlier.
This is where the NHS is failing.

It needs to focus on health, wellbeing and healing, rather than illness, side-effects and suffering.
If you visit someone in hospital, how do you feel when you are in there? I spend quite a lot of time visiting clients in various hospitals and, although the staff are working flat out with the resources they have, the atmosphere is generally depressing. A seriously ill client I was seeing was in a side room right next to the reception desk on the ward. It was so noisy it was impossible to sleep (and sleep is essential for healing). There was very little daylight in the room and you weren't able to open the window as it was locked. It was very stuffy, and the air felt stale.

The whole atmosphere is totally sterile, with no sign of anything natural. You're not allowed flowers or even plants (in case of allergies) even though they are highly beneficial to health.
And the patient is supposed to recover and flourish in this atmosphere?!

A change of emphasis will come in the future, in fact it is already starting.

We are beginning to see alternative therapists working alongside more traditional roles in some hospitals as some of the benefits of holistic care are being witnessed.

This is the path that the NHS is following at the third and highest level, in accordance with divine will. Can you see how the drama being played out at the lower first and second levels, for entirely different reasons, is actually serving the higher agenda?

The more the NHS "fails", the more likely it is that people will look for and embrace complementary therapies alongside existing medical practice. This is an example of how the universe works and it is simply mind blowing!

Let's be quite clear, even with this coming shift in the NHS's focus, we will (at least for the foreseeable future) still need some of the more traditional western medical procedures such as mending broken bones, replacing worn out organs and all the other amazing things consultants can do.

Holistic care is complementary, not an alternative to these incredible surgical skills. Put the two approaches together, working in harmony, and you will have much higher rates of overall success and faster recovery times.

This idea of a lower (first and second railway tracks) and higher (third railway track) agenda can be found throughout society, if you look carefully enough.
Everything is interlinked (remember the hologram), nothing is random and everything is working towards the same goal, even when it appears not to be.

Let's take another example – the still prevalent issue of MPs' expenses!
At level one we have democratically elected people carrying out their public duties and claiming for out-of-pocket expenses in line with the regulations appropriate to their office.

At the second, behind the scenes, level (not as behind the scenes as it used to be, but still there is a great deal of stuff waiting to come out), we have some of those elected representatives claiming for outrageous things and / or inappropriate amounts of money.

Shift to the third level, the divine plan, and the real agenda behind this abuse of public funds becomes apparent;

Politics is not the answer to the world's problems - in fact it's the major factor in creating them and therefore needs to go.

Look around the globe and witness the effects of politics everywhere - disharmony and disunity because the political system is set up to divide people, rather than to bring them together; "United we stand, divided we fall."

The political structure mirrors that of a war with two or more opposing sides. It can never bring people together and it's actually designed specifically not to.

Now, more and more people are seeing through this sham and refusing to play the game. Politicians of all parties have far less power than they used to. Just look at all the U-turns they are increasingly forced into just to cling on to their tenuous positions. It is worth noting that no politicians were invited to the wedding of Prince Harry and Meghan Markle.

It's just a small example of how political power is slowly ebbing away. Politics will disappear if the world is to move forwards and scandals such as the expenses swindle are helping to further undermine politicians' security.

So, although it will no doubt infuriate people that their elected representative has his / her snout in the trough, it's actually a good thing as it is hastening politics' overall demise.

Similarly, if politics has to disappear to move the earth forwards, the last thing we would want to see would-be first-rate politicians being elected. Once again, this negative is really a positive when viewed from the higher perspective. Got it?

Donald Trump is another interesting example.

He is an extreme character- most people either love him or hate him, not many are indifferent to him. This is deliberate. His role is to keep America divided because a divided nation is more easily governed.

Using the three-track model, on track One he has been democratically elected via a transparent election process to lead the country and to pull it together.

Behind the scenes on track Two his election was stage-managed to ensure victory and his job is to keep the nation divided (same as Brexit in the UK).

On track Three, the divine level, he is playing an important role in demonstrating to people the pantomime that is modern day politics, thereby hastening its demise.

Let's take a final example. This one's a biggie - global warming. The hottest day on record, the coldest, the wettest, raging fire storms more intense than any before, the longest drought ever…… you get the picture.

At the level of track One the planet's survival is in real danger due to greenhouse gases from man's industrialisation playing havoc with global temperatures. We are all doomed.

Turning to track Two, behind the scenes this is part of the fear-mongering media machine which is happy to promote the idea of global warming as it keeps people in fear (and therefore suppressed) and they can then enforce carbon footprint tariffs to further penalise the average citizen.

Track Three at last! Global warming is a natural phenomenon and is actually an integral part of the divine plan. In the days of Atlantis, people enjoyed a warm, temperate climate with all of the associated health benefits.

As we continue to ascend to the fifth dimension (see the next chapter), we will leave behind the wild swings in our weather patterns and eventually return to a similar Atlantean climate.

Bring it on!

There you have the three railway tracks. When something in your life seems to be going wrong, whether on the personal level, national or world-wide, try to look for the bigger picture and see whether it is really moving a more important agenda forward. It usually will be.

After a while you will see through most of what's presented to you as truth and life will become much more peaceful and enjoyable, which of course is how it's always meant to have been.

Do try this at home

See if you can apply the three railway tracks model to a story in the national or international news.

Once you get the hang of it, it will become easy to see through much of the negativity put out via the media and to glimpse the divine plan that is the real truth behind it.

14. What on earth is going on?

Following on from the previous chapter, we are now going to look at what is happening globally and beyond and how we all have an equally important role to play.

If you take a quick look at the news stories from around the world, you could easily be forgiven for thinking we are in the middle of a World crisis. As well as "natural" disasters such as earthquakes, wildfires, hurricanes, floods and droughts, we also have the "man-made" stuff going on too such as terrorism, atrocities, starvation, hunger, cancer, corruption etc.

It's certainly not a happy peaceful world we inhabit. Actually, it's all man-made, as we will come to see…

So where do you fit into all of this?

Do you often wonder why am I here? You're not alone if you do. To truly answer that question, we need to look at the purpose of all life as well as your individual life. The universe was created for us to experience all that life is and can be.

Humans were given the divine gift of free will or choice, so we can choose anything and everything in our lives and then experience the effects of our choices. Sometimes we choose things consciously ("I'll have that cake please!") and sometimes unconsciously as already discussed in relation to our health.

Sometimes we choose good things and sometimes bad things.

We are choosing / creating every second we are awake, and the outside world is a perfect mirror reflection of our choices / thoughts. That's why it is so important to watch your thoughts carefully.

When we see a news story detailing the latest terrorist atrocity, we don't for a moment think we are involved in its creation. We think it is solely the responsibility of a distant group of fanatics whose aim is to disrupt our normal lives and of course we condemn their inhumane actions wholeheartedly.

The harsh truth is, however, that we are all to party to, or to "blame" for this outcome ("blame" is the wrong word as it implies judgment and we are not here to judge, but the sense of it is that we are all in part causing the atrocity by what we think and do.).

How can I be causing such misery you will ask?

Well, every time you witness such an event on the TV or elsewhere, you are focusing on it, thereby giving it more energy. What you focus on you create more of, so the photocopier universe sends more of the same stuff that most of us really don't want in the world.

In addition, if the latest atrocity makes us feel angry (of course that's perfectly understandable and appropriate when innocent lives are lost), then we are adding our negative (anger) energy to that of the perpetrators of the crime, again simply increasing the likelihood of more attacks in the future.

In fact, every time we say or think anything negative we are tipping the balance of the world in a downwards direction. This is why every major religion tells us to forgive our enemies. It doesn't mean that we agree with what they are doing - of course we don't - but it means that we invoke the power of love in forgiving and that is the only way to end the seemingly never-ending cycle of killing that the human race has sadly locked itself into for centuries.

It's not just the big news events of the day that we all have an influence on. The little every day interactions we have with people are just as important.

Every time we are kind to someone we are adding to the positive energy in the world.

Even if you just smile at a stranger in the street, or hold the door open, or put a few coins in a homeless person's collecting tin you are putting love out into the world which is the most powerful energy there is.

Don't think for a moment that these small acts of kindness are tiny and therefore relatively ineffective against what's happening globally at the hands of so-called world leaders.

When millions of people around the world are doing similar kind things they add up to an incredibly powerful wave of energy. In fact, they are infinitely more powerful when collated together than anything a politician will ever say or do.
That is how we will "win the war on terrorism" (there's no such thing really, but you get the drift), not by invading countries and killing people to stop *them* killing people (if you want a definition of total insanity this comes pretty close!).

You can't defeat it by focusing on it because in doing so you just give it more energy.

As John Lennon said, "All you need is love." He was right.

We are here to experience life in all its varieties. However, most of us have now truly had enough of experiencing "bad" things over and over again in this life and previous lives and we are really ready to move on.

That's what's happening on the planet right now.

To understand what is really going on, we need to revisit the three railway tracks image from the preceding chapter. At the three-dimensional level, the first rail track, we are in a real mess.

The world's natural resources may have been depleted to a level where they are no longer sustainable.

The planet has been systematically stripped of all of its treasures for profit and greed with little thought of the longer-term consequences.

As one energy source becomes scarce, another is lined up for similar future exploitation such as the relatively new and controversial business of fracking. This process is used to extract shale gas from the earth.
We need to remember that nothing in the universe is random and everything has a role to play and nowhere is this more evident than in nature itself which is delicately balanced in "the circle of life". The gas or liquid trapped in the shale is there for a reason.

I'm no geographical expert but I'd hazard a guess it probably has a role to play in lubricating the plates, hence the tremors that have been experienced near to fracking sites. At the 3D level the world really is in trouble.

At the level of the second track things look equally bleak. Conspiracy theories abound that there is an agenda being pursued relentlessly to keep people as slaves to the system. Lengthy books have been written on this subject, so I am not going to go into detail here. If you want to read about it check out David Icke's books for a thorough, in-depth analysis. Taken in isolation, they are not a pleasant read.

Let's turn to the third track which is the only one that really matters in the end. There are amazing things happening here.
The world is being helped to ascend from 3D consciousness to 5D as part of the Divine Plan.

What on earth does that mean?

It means that sufficient people on the planet have woken up to the lies they have been subjected to for so long and change is finally happening.
If you look around you can see signs of it. The Hollywood sex scandal is one example. It's only the tip of the iceberg but the truth is finally emerging.

Corruption in Governments and the big corporations is also emerging. Equal pay for women in the BBC is one small example. It is difficult to understand how a male and female presenter doing the same job on the same programme can still be paid such widely differing salaries in this day and age, but they are.

Child grooming and paedophilia across the UK – and the US - is being unearthed systematically.

Cheating and corruption in most sports has been discovered and publicised.

Finally, action is being taken to reduce plastic pollution in the oceans. There is much more negativity to come out before the planet ascends, but we are at last on our way.

Why is the world in such a state in the three-dimensional plane?

The planet has suffered for centuries from too much emphasis being placed on masculine energy to the detriment of feminine energy. As in the natural world, they need to be in balance and harmony if the world is to move upwards. This is true both of the individual human being and the planet as a whole. One is not better than the other - they are interconnected, they are complementary.

The feminine values of nurturing, caring and loving are essential for the world to be balanced alongside the more masculine values related primarily to strength and protection.

What is going to happen as we ascend?

No-one really knows because we are at the cutting edge here. This has not been attempted anywhere else in the universe previously.

We are literally making it up as we go along through our creative thoughts.
I believe there are other civilisations on other planets far ahead of us,

but nowhere has the transition been made from a relatively low level three-dimensional physical world to the more spiritual fifth dimension, as we are doing.

How do you fit into this?

You chose to be a part of this before you incarnated on the planet. You have had many previous lives and decided to return at this point in the earth's history to help with the divine plan. You probably won't remember making that conscious choice to be here now because part of the deal is that we forget where we came from and why until we begin to wake up later in life or when we again return home at the moment of what we call "death".

This amnesia is required so that we can experience everything in life in its richness and fullness. If we saw through it straight away, it would be nowhere near as powerful an experience. Remember the magician sawing the woman in half?

There are many advanced souls here on the planet at this present time who have also chosen to donate their experience and knowledge to help the planet to ascend at this time. Some are famous and well known, leading from the front, and others are unknown, working quietly but effectively in the background.

All are equally important and powerful. If this book is resonating with you, then you may well be one of them.

So how do you help in the transition? Well, it works on different levels.

Remember what I said about putting out positive energy. Every time you do that you are assisting the global push to ascension. Every time you put out negative energy you are hindering the process.

Every time you carry out an act of kindness you are helping, every time you gossip, slander or abuse someone you are hindering.

It's not just actions that carry that energy, it's also your thoughts so think well of people as often as you can, no matter what they think or do. Practice forgiveness.

Next time a politician does something that makes you angry, instead of ranting about it for days afterwards, instead think "I truly hope he / she will learn from that experience and will act in a way that moves the world forwards next time."

If someone hurts you, remember that they are just further behind you on the path to enlightenment, in exactly the same place where you were several lives ago. That doesn't make you better than them, just more awake. They will get there eventually, no matter how long it takes, simply because there is nowhere else to get to.

Follow your passion in life, whatever it is. Then you will find it easy to be positive, happy, joyful and peaceful and in this way, you will be helping the world to move forwards.

It might help you to understand all this more fully if we dip a toe briefly into the mysterious murky waters that make up quantum physics. Don't worry, it's only a toe!

Scientists have had to accept that the universe is really nothing like what they thought it was until very recently. Perhaps the most important aspect to grasp is that the universe and everything in it does not really exist outside of us - it's just a hologram. In fact, it is a projection from our minds.

We are literally projecting a film from our mind which is coloured by our beliefs and thoughts, which then appears as our reality on the screen of life. So not only do our thoughts affect the outside world, they are in reality *creating* it. If we didn't exist, neither would the world as there would be nobody in the projection room.

Following this through to its logical conclusion, we have no-one to blame for the state of the world but ourselves, as I said earlier in relation to terrorist activities, as it is our film for which we are the director, producer and we also star in it as actors. Remember what Shakespeare said?

"All the world's a stage, And all the men and women merely players; They have their exits and their entrances; And one man in his time plays many parts..."
(As you like it)

You can dry your toe off now with your towel. What is needed to move the world upwards is a revolution, but not an external revolution as those have been proved time and time again to only be a temporary fix at best.

No, we need an internal revolution in each person's mind so that love becomes the normal response to every incident in everyone's lives.

The world would then change because we would have loaded a brand-new film into the projector.

No more "horror" movies!

You don't need leaders to make laws ordering you to do this. It starts right here right now with you!

Do try this at home

Try to put into practice forgiveness and kindness in all that you see, hear and do.

Lose the anger at what you see going on around the world and instead help to spread positivity.

Fulfil the mission you agreed to carry out when you incarnated on the planet by doing what you love to do.

15. Is there a Future for Religion?

As the world ascends to the 5th dimensional level, some things will either cease to exist or will have to change radically if they are to survive there. Why?

You will recall that everything is made of energy. This energy vibrates at various frequencies and as we ascend the speed of vibration will increase.

Anything with a slow rate of vibration simply cannot exist at these higher planes of existence. Generally, it is the worst of human behaviour that vibrates at the slower rates, such as crime, war, hatred, greed, corruption and so on. This climb to 5D is where the idea of heaven on earth (the kingdom) comes from as there will be no place for these.

Let's examine one aspect of human existence that is already facing the choice of either changing radically or disappearing forever – Religion.

Religion and I parted company at an early age.

I just couldn't get my head around the idea of a God who is supposedly all love sending his only son to be sacrificed in the worst way imaginable for the sins of the world so that God would then be "reconciled" to the world again.

What kind of Father would do such a thing to his "beloved son"?

It never made any sense to me and it's not surprising as, of course, it's total nonsense, put out by the church authorities over the centuries to keep the common people in fear and submission.

If you want to read a far more likely account of the meaning of the life of Jesus, then try **"The Transmigrant" by Kristi Saare Duarte** which I thoroughly recommend.

Churches in the UK are struggling to keep going in many places. They have a rapidly ageing and dwindling congregation and have tried all kinds of things to entice younger worshippers in (messy church, for example). Nothing seems to work.

Contrast that with the way people of all ages and backgrounds flocked to hear Jesus or the Buddha or other great spiritual masters speak. They didn't need messy church or even a building to preach in and were enormously popular. What's gone wrong? Why isn't church working?

It's simple. All of the great spiritual leaders spoke their truth. They spoke from the heart. They didn't need to threaten or bully people to get them to listen. People were drawn to them because truth always resonates with people, as we have discussed many times already in this book.

Let's be clear about what religion is.

It's essentially a set of man-made rules and each different religion has its own set, each proclaiming that theirs is the right way and all the others are wrong or at least inferior to theirs. Which set of rules (if any) you choose to follow depends largely upon where you live, and which set your family follows.

As religions have sprung up and developed over the centuries, they have generally drifted further and further away from the original truths as taught by the great spiritual masters.

At a subconscious level, or even conscious now for many people, they recognise that they are not being given the truth by their religion. It doesn't resonate with them, so they don't feel drawn to it and therefore choose not to take part or to go to church.

Why would you do something you don't enjoy if you don't have to? To understand what's really going on behind this we need to return once again to the three railway tracks model.

At the physical world level of Track One we have religions supposedly established to guide people along the way. To show them how to live and how to connect with God through them. We have churches and other holy buildings built to give all people a safe haven where they can worship in peace, away from the distractions of the outside world under the guidance of the spiritual hierarchy.

At the second (underground) level, church authorities over the centuries have distorted the original truths spoken by the spiritual masters, perhaps sometimes unintentionally and sometimes deliberately to suit their own aims.

They have deliberately omitted certain things from their religion's sacred texts and also added their own "facts" to suit their agenda. Transforming Mary Magdalene from Jesus' chief disciple into a former prostitute is a good example of how the church has been prepared to distort, to simply make things up.

In this case the idea was to dumb down women's roles in their structure, so the men could keep all the power. Paying for your sins and spending time in something called purgatory are further examples of similar fiction to keep people in fear. The ordinary man's connection to God is severed by the Church claiming it alone has direct contact with God.

People are forced to buy into the Church to "look after their soul". At the divine third level, not surprisingly, all is going to plan. More and more people are seeing through the deceptions outlined above, hence church attendance is at an all-time low in the UK.

This was predicted by John Lennon in 1966 when he said "Christianity will go. It will vanish and shrink." which caused uproar in America but has proved to be accurate in the UK at least. In his song "Imagine" he sings of a world with no religion. There is no doubt that this is what is coming because...

Religion is politics for the soul and it has run its course.

Churches, as they have been set up, are a barrier to God, not a gateway. They are a wall, not a bridge. This was brought home to me a few years ago when I was talking to two friends who, I found out, used to do healing having been trained in Reiki.

"So why did you stop?" I asked.
"Oh, well, er, our minister didn't approve of us doing "healing", so we stopped. We used to love doing it."

I came up against a similar brick wall when I offered to give free healing to anyone in a local hospice who wanted to try some, whether patients or staff.

Despite meeting with the pastor, who promised to get back to me, I never heard anything. After that I contacted the same hospice five more times but didn't even get a letter or an email back saying no thank-you.

I mention this not because my ego is hurt by the rejection, but because it's an example of why religion is a barrier, not a gateway to God, as I said above. The act of healing is about as Christian an activity as you can get. Didn't Jesus send his disciples out to heal people and weren't they ordinary people, fishermen and the like?

Why should any individual (in this case a church minister) decide that healing is not appropriate for somebody else, without even asking their own opinion on it?

If you or your child had a terminal illness and you found out that somebody had decided to say no to free treatment for you, without even consulting you, how would you feel about it?

Everyone has the right to choose for themselves in my world and if they choose to decline the offer then of course I will respect their decision. It's their decision to make, not someone else's. As the planet ascends to the fifth dimension, there will be no room for this kind of divisive negative thinking.

We are all equal because we are all one.

We all have access to divine guidance wherever we are and don't need a religious "specialist" to do the work or to make arbitrary decisions for us.

I've just had one of those coincidental happenings I've talked about earlier which I'm including as it's directly concerned with what we are talking about here. It's Easter week-end and I'm typing away in the kitchen when there's a knock at the door. I open it and there are two men stood there. I'm not going to mention to which religious group they belonged as it's unimportant and the exchange below would probably have been similar with devotees of most groups.

"Good morning! I'm here to talk to you about the true meaning of Easter!" said one of the men.

He had come to tell me his account of the second coming and how only those chosen would be lifted up to heaven.
I listened briefly and then said;
"Didn't Jesus say that all are welcome at my Father's table? And didn't he say that the Kingdom of God is within you?"

The two men had come to convert people to their beliefs, not to listen to others so they very soon departed when they realised I wasn't a likely candidate. I mention this incident not to knock anyone's religion (all are entitled to their own beliefs), but to demonstrate how limited their viewpoints often are – believing that our way is the only right way.

This is why religion in its current state has no future.

If religion is going to disappear, or change, what, if anything, is going to take its place?

People need to have a meaning to their lives, otherwise they are empty and stuck in the material world where happiness is always short-lived because it depends upon having and keeping "things". This is how many people in the Western world are currently living their lives and they are not really happy. The nearest I can think of to describe what will replace religion is "spiritual awareness". What do I mean by this?

People will eventually re-connect with God both on an individual and mass consciousness basis without the need for a set of religious rules to do so.

In fact, there is no need to re-connect because that connection has been there all the time - it never left- people just think it did and as we know so well by now, what you think you create in your world. It would be more accurate to say that people will remember their connection with God and begin to use it again. But not in the old ways of worshipping and begging for forgiveness for sins and so on.

The new relationship with the divine will be more like the experiences described in this book.

People will rediscover the divine potential within themselves, rather than as an external omniscient deity who may or may not grant your request depending upon how many sins you've committed and how "he" is feeling on that particular day.

People will finally understand what Jesus meant when he said: "The Kingdom of God is within you".

Will we still have leaders in this brave new world? Yes, absolutely we will, but leaders won't govern in the future, instead they will lead by example.

Rather than being told what to do and punished if they don't toe the line, people will voluntarily choose to live their lives like those who inspire them.

Life will be full of joy and laughter.

The world has been far too serious a place for too long.

I love the page in Neale Walsch's "Conversations with God" when God cracks a joke and Neale says "Hey, aren't you supposed to be sombre and serious, bearing in mind who you are?" God answers "Oh yeah? And who do you think invented humour!"

This is one of the things I think religion has really lost out on. Going to church is hardly a barrel of laughs, is it? There is absolutely nothing wrong with humour. It is not irreverent. Humour is spiritual - it makes you feel good. That's why half the population of this country used to watch the Morecambe and Wise Christmas show. It was pure joy.

It was two grown men behaving in a way we all wished we could behave and not only getting away with it but even being paid to do it. Laughter really is the best medicine.

Why do you think so many of the effigies of Buddha show him laughing heartily?
Maybe God had just told him a joke?

On my own spiritual journey there are many times when humour has suddenly appeared in the most unlikely of situations. Here are a few...

I was giving some healing to a friend who had had a skiing accident, leaving him with a badly swollen knee joint. As I was administering hands-on healing on his knee he started thrashing around with his leg.

"Sorry!" I said, "Is that painful?"
"No!" he managed to blurt out, "I'm being tickled!"

I took some flowers to the local crematorium recently where there is a memorial stone for my mother-in-law who died some time ago.

It was a rainy day and I had my hood up to keep dry. I got to her stone and started to cut the flowers to fit into the pot there and to generally tidy up what was already there.

The hood on my coat is a bit too big for my head so it kept flopping over my eyes so I couldn't see what I was doing very well.

There is a plastic butterfly on a stick with a suitable loving message, which my wife had left there, in the pot which kept getting in the way.
Every time I pushed it to the one side to allow me to arrange the flowers, a sudden gust of wind blew it back. After this had happened three times, I lifted my hood up a bit to have a proper look and laughed out loud.

The butterfly's stick was in the pot belonging to the stone next to the one I had started to fill, and I was putting the flowers in the wrong pot, thanks to my hood being over my eyes. "At last!" I heard a laughing voice say in my head.

A friend and I were doing a joint healing session on another friend in a room at our house. It was before I had a separate music studio so in the room there was also a drum kit and other musical stuff.

In the middle of the healing there was a loud crash as somebody hit the snare drum. There was nobody visible, but somebody had decided to announce their invisible presence. After we'd finished the healing, our friend sat up and said: "Did you hear that crash?" "Yes." said my co-healer, "It was me. I asked for whoever was in the room to make themselves known!"

Recently I've been doing some decorating for my son and his girlfriend, who have bought their first house.

I was upstairs in one of the bedrooms doing some wallpapering, alone in the house. I used my steel tape measure to mark off the next piece of paper to be cut to size and then used it as a paperweight to stop the roll of wallpaper from rolling itself up again while I was cutting it.

As I was half way across with the scissors, the tape fell onto the floor under the pasting table I was working on. Could I find it? No matter where I looked it had simply disappeared.

Eventually, I did find it on the other side of the room and completely hidden underneath a bag of rubbish.

Now there is no way it could have rolled over there as it's square, not round, and even if it had been round how could it get under a bag of rubbish? Somebody was playing a trick on me.

Ha! You won't believe this but while I was sitting in the lounge typing this there has suddenly been a similar noise right in front of me, as if something had fallen onto a drum. Trouble is there's no drum in the lounge and nothing has fallen down!

Like I said, humour is spiritual.

While doing healings I have been prodded in the chest, patted on the head and had my hair ruffled, all by invisible hands. It's all good fun. It goes with the territory.

So, if religion is to survive, it will have to embrace great change, stop dictating to people how they should live their lives, start leading by example by sharing out its wealth with the poor and lighten up! Let's see what happens...

Do try this at home

Read **"The Transmigrant" by Kristi Saare Duarte**!

16. Death is vastly over-rated!

Here we are at the end. Already. That's gone so quickly! What better topic to finish off with than the final destination...except it isn't, of course. Why?

Because there's no such thing as death.

I could finish this chapter there, after all, what else is there to say of any value about something that doesn't exist? Well, considering it's a work of fiction, most people spend an awful lot of time worrying and / or in fear of it so maybe we ought to delve a little deeper. So here goes...

I know that death doesn't exist because I've been "dead" and returned to what we call life.

In my case it wasn't a "near death experience" like many that have been reported, it was quite different. It happened when I was at junior school. I was 11 years old and it was the end of the school day. I was on my way home on foot and a friend and I were playing "tick". He was chasing me along the path as we got to the main road where the school crossing patrol was situated.

I was more concerned about not being caught by my friend than anything to do with road safety. As I glanced out of the corner of my eye, I was sure the crossing lady was standing in the middle of the road with the "lollipop" in her hand, so it was safe to cross, but I didn't look properly. I ran out into the road straight into the path of an oncoming car that had no possible chance of stopping in time.

I heard the screech of his brakes and felt the car just start to touch me ....
The next thing I remember I was walking away on the other side of the road, looking back shakily as the driver angrily honked his horn and the crossing lady shouted to me "You stupid boy! Don't you ever do that again!"

At the time I remember thinking "How did that happen?" I knew I had been hit by the car and I knew that somehow, I had been placed on the other side of the road without a scratch?

I had no idea how that could happen. As I was only 11 years old, I soon forgot about it and put it down to "just one of those things". I didn't tell anybody about my experience. My parents would have been livid and my friend who had been chasing me thought I'd just had a narrow escape...but I knew differently.

I forgot all about it for many years. After my spiritual awakening some 40 years later, that incident kept reappearing in my mind so eventually I asked for help from my spirit guides in understanding what really happened that day.

It was explained to me that we all have a number of agreed "exit" points in our life when we are given the option of leaving the planet and returning home. We have the choice.

As I have already said earlier, nothing in the universe is random, including what we call death. Most people will only choose to leave when they feel they have completed whatever task their higher self-took on in this lifetime.

There are exceptions to this, of course, including some who choose to take their own lives.

Of course, this "choosing to leave" is a difficult concept to take on board when a relatively young person dies or a parent leaves behind young children and so on.

In earthly terms, of course they haven't finished their work - how could they have done when for instance their young children no longer have a parent to look after them?

This will never make sense if you only look at life from a limited 3D perspective.

To understand it, you have to take a wider view. The parent may have chosen to experience leaving behind their young family as part of their life purpose, and the children may have chosen to experience living without a parent as part of their own spiritual growth.

Nothing is random - it is all part of a complex web of relationships that inter-weave and affect each other. But why on earth would they choose that, you will ask, as it will be such a painful experience?

Well, if they had already lived many previous lifetimes within a fully functioning happy family unit, they might decide to experience something different this time, in order to then fully appreciate the blessings they had enjoyed previously in their families.

Sometimes you don't fully appreciate something until it's no longer there.
Of course, for those family members left behind on earth, a death is an intensely painful experience and I do not intend to trivialise that in any way as I went through the full range of emotions myself when my sister died "prematurely". However, choosing a life path is really no different to any other choices you make in your life.

You may absolutely love Honda cars, for example, and buy one after another because they offer you everything you want in a car.

One day you will decide to try another car just to see what it's like, just to see if the Honda really is as good as you think, just to give you something to compare it with. It's exactly the same with life choices.

If you've experienced joy and happiness in lifetime after lifetime you will eventually decide to try something more challenging for all the reasons outlined above. This is especially true as you climb the ascension ladder and gain spiritual wisdom.
The further you climb, the more challenging the experiences will be to give you the required depth of experience. So, the more advanced you are spiritually, the more difficult your life will appear to be to others...*but not to you!*

This is also often true for people with so-called disabilities.

Many are advanced souls with experience of many previous lives as healthy, fully able people and they have now chosen to experience life in a different way. The last thing they want from us is pity - instead they deserve our admiration. And so do their parents who have equally chosen this sometimes-challenging experience for their own spiritual growth.

The other thing to bear in mind is that the person returning home "early" is only leaving the three- dimensional world behind. They are still multi-dimensional and experiencing life with the same family members in other dimensions, so they haven't really left them at all, they're just not experiencing the three-dimensional aspect of their relationship any longer.

At some point in the future they may all decide to try the 3D experience again with the same family members, maybe swopping roles this time so the child becomes the mother, the brother becomes the sister and so on.

I believe the road incident was one of my own exit points.

I was actually killed by the car and went "home".

I hadn't even started on my life purpose by that age, however, so I was allowed to return to earth seconds after I was hit by the car, so no-one would suspect anything had happened. Remember that where we come from there is no such thing as time, so it is easy to just reappear seconds later. I have no memory of being "dead" because in returning to this planet I went through the veils of amnesia again as previously discussed.

I obviously had another exit point just after the Liverpool incident as you will recall I was again given the option of leaving but decided to stay to see out my mission.

I have since learned that everyone has three or four exit points in their lives. Often you will hear of someone having a near miss or a lucky escape and these are sometimes exit points where the person has chosen to stay.

Conversely, sometimes people seem to leave in the unlikeliest of scenarios and people often say: "It was just their time to go."

That is exactly right. If the soul is ready to depart, it will always find a way to engineer an exit strategy from this planet.

I believe that the process behind my return to this life after I was run over by a car was very similar to that which brought Jesus back "from the dead" after his crucifixion. Every time he performed a miracle, he was always at pains to explain to his disciples that *they* would do all he could do and more. I do believe that he died on the cross, as planned, and was returned to the 3D world three earth days later.

So, let's move on to talk about reincarnation now.

If you've ever heard the song **"The Circle Game"** recorded by **Joni Mitchell**, amongst others, you will have heard a perfect summary of the reincarnation process to date. The lyrics include;

"We're captive on the carousel of time
We can't return we can only look behind
From where we came
And go around and round and round
In the circle game."

Without wishing to focus on negatives, this has been how the world has operated for a very long time. We finish one lifetime only to start another still stuck in the three-dimensional plane with little chance of progressing upwards to higher planes.

So, what happened to our free will and choice?

It was essentially subverted by outside interference from other dimensions.

Again, if you want to know more read David Icke and others. The important point for this book though is that this has now run its course, thanks partly to people like David who were brave enough to reveal the truth to a dubious world, and to other outside help we are receiving from beyond the planet.

We are now free to progress spiritually, if we choose to do so, and many are. Others are choosing not to ascend and to leave this planet instead. You will no doubt have noticed how many from the music and entertainment worlds have died in the last few years.

At the soul level this is their own choice. They have enjoyed their three-dimensional life so much that they do not wish to ascend further at this stage, so they will instead choose to incarnate on another 3D planet similar to Earth elsewhere in the universe and then explore another aspect of life there as a physical being.

This does not make them somehow inferior to others who are ascending. It is simply them exercising their free will. At some point they will eventually tire of 3D life and choose to progress further, but it is entirely up to them to decide when to do so.

It's a bit like playing Monopoly. You may enjoy having hotels on Park Lane and winning game after game, but eventually you will get bored and want to play a different game. So it is with life on Earth.

There has been a lot of stuff written about reincarnation and there is a lot of confusion surrounding the topic. I will try to explain my understanding of it.

First, it's both correct and incorrect to say that in a previous life you were so and so. "I thought you were going to clarify it?" I hear you say. "That's not helping!" Think of it this way...Imagine the soul being like an onion.

If you peel a layer off the onion it is both an individual part of the onion but also still contains the essence of the whole onion. It has an equal amount of "onionness" in it as it contains everything that the whole onion contains, so although it has been separated from the whole it remains a part of it.

Think of the soul in the same way. Every so often a layer peels off and becomes a new life on earth (or elsewhere). It is only a part of the soul, but it contains the core essence of everything that the whole soul contains.

Each soul has acquired knowledge from its previous life experiences which the new person incarnating brings with him / her at a subconscious level.

When **Mozart** came to the planet, he was able to draw on many previous lifetimes as a musician and appeared to be a child genius, composing from the age of five.
He subsequently reappeared as another child prodigy many years later when another layer from the same soul peeled off and he incarnated as pop idol **Michael Jackson**!

Bold claim I hear you say. Prove it! Of course, I cannot offer "real-world-evidence" but I KNOW this to be true. How do I know? I get told by my spirit helpers, usually when I am carrying out a healing and my mind is in a meditative state. I never just accept it, though, and always ask for some kind of confirmation to ensure as far as possible that it is the truth.

This usually appears in the form of a synchronicity such as the person in question being mentioned as soon as I switch the TV on, or something similar. I have already mentioned similar synchronicities with clients and their past lives and to date no one has seen fit to argue with me.

As I said earlier, it is difficult to argue with the truth. Perhaps I will explain more, as much as I can explain, in a follow-up book.

Often people choose to follow a certain theme or occupation across many lifetimes to hone their skills further.

The popular singer **Adele**, for example, previously "lived" as **(Mama) Cass Elliott** of the sixty's harmony group **The Mamas and the Papas**. Her song "Hello" even contains references to this, which she may not be consciously aware of, as we discussed earlier in this book, but her subconscious is of course fully aware of it.

She sings "Hello from the other side." (big clue there!) and "I'm in California dreaming about who we used to be - When we were younger and free."
"California Dreaming" was of course The Mamas and the Papas' biggest hit when Adele was indeed "younger" and living in California.

When I was a teenager trying to learn how to play lead guitar my hero was **Richie Blackmore** of the rock band **Deep Purple**. I couldn't believe how good he was.

It didn't seem humanly possible to move your fingers that quickly and try as I might I could never come close. I understand now that he was clearly also a guitarist in a previous life or, more likely, lives so it came relatively easily to him.

After a highly successful career as a rock guitarist, Richie confounded public expectations by then forming an acoustic outfit playing medieval music.
Yes, no doubt he was revisiting one of his past lives as a wandering minstrel playing the string instruments of that time such as the lute and the lyre!

Another example of someone pursuing similar interests across lifetimes is **Richard Arkwright** who was highly influential as an inventor in the early industrial revolution in the UK.
After his death he soon returned to continue his engineering work and to refine his expertise still further when he incarnated as **Isambard Kingdom Brunel**.

TV personality **Jonathan Ross** is known for his clever wordplay and quick wit, which he refined in his previous existence as the celebrated Irish poet and playwright **Oscar Wilde**.

When I was given this information, it was immediately reinforced when I picked up a TV guide shortly afterwards to find a photo of Jonathan on one page and one of Oscar on the very next! And they do look remarkably similar in their facial features.

Orchestral maestro **Andre Rieu** has a passion for the waltz. It's not surprising as one of his previous lifetimes was as Viennese composer **Johann Strauss**.

Comedian **Russell Brand** sports long hair and leather trousers and has lived a rock star-like life of excess involving drugs. His previous life was as **Jim Morrison**, lead singer with the group **The Doors** and he is clearly still working his way through some of the same issues that destroyed him at that time.

Ironically, Russell has even played a rock star in a film. Old habits are sometimes hard to break.

In other cases, someone may choose to live a completely different sort of life from one extreme to another to broaden their experience.

In **"Viva la Vida" by Coldplay, Chris Martin** is singing about two previously contrasting lifetimes of his - one where he was a King who "ruled the world" and another where he sweeps the streets.

This is a good example of the soul choosing to experience the full extremes of life's possibilities. "Viva la Vida" is, appropriately, Spanish for "Long live Life". The clue is there in the title.

Kate Bush previously incarnated as **Anne Boleyn** and if you watch her video for her song "The Sensual World" you will see her dressed very like Anne and dancing through a forest using movements that come from that time period.

In other words, she is subconsciously enjoying reliving a part of her past history.

I mentioned earlier that we went to see **Beverley Craven** in concert. I had actually met her some years before when she was a guest speaker at a song writing conference I attended. What a lovely lady! I have since seen her in one of her previous lives when she was Dinah, daughter of Jacob in the Old Testament.

How come all these people have been famous in previous lives, you may ask? Although all lives are sacred and, therefore, equally important whether famous or unknown, it is quite common for people who rise to the top of their chosen path to be equally successful or influential in certain subsequent lifetimes, even where they are pursuing very different careers.

French **Queen Marie Antoinette** enchanted the courts with her lively wit before she fell out of favour and met her untimely end.
This same quality was again evident when she reincarnated as **Marilyn Monroe**, the American actress and sex symbol.
Beneath the glitz and the glamour of both lives, there is a very similar story of unhappiness and loneliness and an early exit from the planet.

Of course, it's not just people who have done "good" things in their lives that return to the planet over and over again.
Those who have chosen to pursue "evil" as we would understand it, will also reincarnate to learn the lessons they have so far failed to take on board.

Sometimes they seem to be making little progress in their spirituality. **Adolf Hitler's** illogical and unfounded hatred of the Jews is more easily understood when you realise that one of his previous lives was as **Pontius Pilate**, the Roman who sentenced Jesus to death and who persecuted the Jews of that time mercilessly.

Sometimes a person undergoes a dramatic event in their life and the memory of this still reverberates in successive lifetimes, even though the person may not be consciously aware of their previous life.

For example, American singer / songwriter **Paul Simon** sings about a journey he undertook in 1620 in his song "American Tune".
The song presents a very personal insight into the trials of being one of the pilgrims who sailed from Plymouth on the Mayflower to the New World.

Paul revisits a similar theme in his song "America" in which all the people he sees have all come to look for America.

When the person "dies" they do not cease to exist as the person they were, but continue as the same multi-dimensional individual, only without a physical presence here on Earth.

When Brunel died, he would have been able to meet Arkwright and discuss his work with him. Both would feel that they knew each other, had met each other before but would not be sure when or how, because in essence they are different aspects of the same soul.

They are the exact same soul but have experienced life on earth in different physical bodies, as two separate layers of the onion. They would each recognise themselves in the other person, whilst simultaneously remaining separate.

Another way of looking at it is to say that Brunel would never find anybody else so closely matched to himself as a previous life than Arkwright, unless they were yet another person from the same soul.

Are we generally meant to be aware of our previous lives? No, not really.
Can you imagine trying to live a normal life with your human head full of experiences, opinions and thoughts from several hundred previous existences?!

It would be impossible. Instead we get the odd instance of déjà vu or similar to just give us a nudge as to the true nature of reality.

I hope that explains it sufficiently!

Bold claims I hear you say again! And again, there is no specific "real-world-evidence" but, as explained earlier, I KNOW this to be true. As with all of the content in this book, you are entirely free to take on board those aspects that resonate with you and to discard anything that you can't buy into.

If *you* find it difficult to believe this aspect of life you may find it helpful to be aware of numerous experiments carried out with young children who were questioned in laboratory conditions about some of their previous lives.
The children were able to give remarkably detailed explanations of places they had never visited in their current lifetimes which were later validated as completely accurate.

The reason for this is that children still retain a good deal of knowledge about their previous lives, as they have not yet been fully conditioned by the world to forget who they really are.

As they become adults they lose more and more of this knowledge as they are submerged in the bewildering 3D experience that we call life on earth and block out memories and experiences which don't fit in with what they see around them.

I sometimes carry out past life regressions with some clients who come for healing. In some cases they are simply curious to know "who they were" in a previous life, but in others it can be a very useful tool to remove illness, anxiety or negativity that they are still carrying around with them.

I have found that the best way to do this is to give hands on healing whilst firstly talking the client through a relaxation meditation. Once the client is fully relaxed, I then take them through the regression exercise, giving healing at all times.

In this way, not only is the client able to re-visit an episode which is still troubling them in order to resolve it, but also I am simultaneously sending healing back into that past life to help them deal with it. This usually produces a very positive outcome.

So why are we so scared of death if there really is nothing to fear?

Well, most people have lived many lives and carry with them in their subconscious all that they have experienced in those lives. If, for example, you have lived through a period of history when the concept of hell, eternal damnation and Satan was not only promoted by your religion, but widely believed by most people, you can imagine the fear you lived with in case you did anything wrong.

And it would have been quite easy to do something wrong because the rules governing what was right were deliberately too complex for the average person to even begin to understand so the churches could guarantee a healthy trade in forgiving sins.

Add to this the fact that the church deliberately removed the many references to reincarnation that were originally in the Bible to maintain its position of power and authority over the common people (there are still a few to be found in the Old Testament that were overlooked.).

How could you burn in everlasting fires of hell if you sinned, if you could also reincarnate as a new human being!?
You get the idea. It didn't fit with their agenda to keep people in fear, so the concept was erased, they simply got rid of it.

The world has promoted the fear of death through religion and nowadays largely through the media, as religion has declined in its influence over the majority, at least in the UK.

The truth is that death is really like opening a door and going from one room into another.

This was Jesus' true purpose - to demonstrate that even the most horrible form of death is meaningless because life is eternal.

It's time to stop worrying about death and to really start living. Viva la Vida!

Do try this at home

Don't worry, be happy!

Understand that death is just another three-dimensional lie like so many others we have looked at in this book.

17. Lola Bleu

"Life is what happens to you while you're busy making plans" John Lennon said.

Oh so true. Life is in constant motion. Life is change. We never know what's just around the corner and sometimes it's just as well. I thought I'd finished writing this book, but then my whole world was turned upside down...again....

We were happily awaiting the birth of our first grand-daughter, eagerly anticipating a moment of extreme joy and gratitude.
Our daughter was a week overdue when she went into labour.

I am not going to go into detail but suffice to say that after a lengthy period of labour she was finally rushed to theatre for an emergency caesarean section. The baby wasn't breathing and went straight into intensive care. She was dangerously ill for the next two days and our world was rocked from top to bottom.

It is the most painful thing in the world to watch your own child suffering intensely as you feel helpless to intervene, at least on the physical level.

Obviously, I was sending healing to the baby at every opportunity and asking other healers to do the same. On the third day thankfully, there was some limited improvement and slowly over the next week the clouds started to lift.

As I write this she has just come out of the incubator and is now gaining weight and looking beautiful. We are truly blessed.

I have decided to include this because it pulls together so many of the ideas presented in this book.

Throughout the experience I did my best to remain focused on a positive outcome for the baby.

That doesn't mean that I found it easy. It was very challenging at times, particularly when things weren't improving.

Nevertheless, I kept visualising our daughter bringing home a healthy happy baby.

The care and expertise given by the staff at the hospital was amazing. You have to be special to face the challenges presented by new-borns on a daily basis.

We will be forever grateful for their love and care and their total professionalism. However, I am also very aware of the help we were given from beyond the physical world. I was, of course, giving the baby healing whenever possible, albeit secretly as I did not wish to risk being evicted from the unit by the professional staff.

I felt the power of healing flooding through my hands and said many thank-yous in my mind for this wonderful gift. When you put Western medical excellence alongside spiritual healing you can achieve phenomenal outcomes.

They are complementary practices. This is a great example of how the NHS could work in the future.

Many of our friends were also sending healing in their own ways and I have felt a tremendous wave of love surrounding us during the most difficult times.

We have had literally hundreds of messages of goodwill from friends near and far, raising the love vibration around the world, thereby helping the planet to ascend to the next level. This is the impact of a single tiny helpless baby coming into the world and facing difficulties.

She has already made a difference and at the time of writing she is only a week old.

I have watched with awe at the way my daughter and her partner have dealt with what life has thrown at them.

They have grown so much over the last week and are ready to move on to whatever life now holds in store for them.

They are already amazing parents.

There are no coincidences in life, and everything happens for a reason. I smiled to myself when one of the staff on the unit said to us "I'm not religious, but I believe God never gives anybody more than they can cope with at any time".

I have been reminded about the importance of our human relationships. Nothing is more important than caring for each other. All the wealth in the world is meaningless next to the value of a child's life.
Sometimes we forget this simple truth and life reminds us in painful ways.
What you put out into the world will always come back to you. The healing I have given to people over the years has been more than repaid a thousand times over by my tiny grand-daughter's return to health. The photocopier universe never runs out of paper or ink.

My own spiritual journey has been significantly enhanced by the experience we have just been through.
The voice I first heard in Liverpool all those years ago is finally back and guiding me on a daily basis.
I have been told that this connection is now permanent as I have grown sufficiently in a spiritual sense to maintain it.

We have come full circle in this book which began with my awakening in Liverpool and ends with another significant milestone in my life journey. I am totally excited about what is next to come in my life.

This is just another effect of my beautiful grand-daughter's arrival on the planet. Thank-you Lola!

18. And in the end...

And in the end the love you take
Is equal to the love you make.

Those are the last two lines of side two of the Beatles final album "Abbey Road" (apart from the throwaway clip from "Her Majesty" which ends the record.).

"Let it Be" was released after "Abbey Road" but was actually recorded before it. It is a simple but profound statement - in life you get given exactly what you give out.
Everything is in perfect balance.
It summarises how life works in 15 words.

Why do people have to make everything so complicated? If everyone on the planet took this simple message on board and lived by it, then we would indeed bring heaven to earth.

I hope you have enjoyed reading this short book and found something of value in it for you. As I said at the beginning, just take what works for you from it and reject the rest.

That is **YOUR** choice!
May your current life and future lives be filled with joy and happiness!

Peace be with you.
Keith Forrest

Postscript: During the process of publishing, I sensed the need to expand on the themes and examples within this book and to add to my personal insight and experiences.
If you have made it this far you may be delighted to learn that Book 2 is currently in production although a title and launch date are yet to be confirmed.
If you want to be kept informed of progress and launch simply visit
www.keithforrest.co.uk **Until the next time!**

Bibliography

Byrne, Lorna. *Angels in my Hair.* Random House, 2008.

Byrne, Rhonda. *The Secret.* Aria Publishing Group. Beyond Words Publishing, 2006.

Downey, Roma. *Box of Butterflies: Discovering the Unexpected Blessings all around us.* Howard Books, 2018.

Duarte, Kristi Saare. *The Transmigrant.* Conspicuum Press. 2017.

Dyer, Wayne. Change your Thoughts, change your Life: Living the Wisdom of the Tao. Hay House. 2007.

Hicks, Esther and Jerry. *Ask and it is Given: Learning to Manifest your desires.* Hay House Publishing, 2004.

Tolle, Eckhart. Practising the Power of Now: A Guide to Spiritual Enlightenment. Namaste Publishing, New World Library. 1997.

Walsch, Neale Donald. *Conversations with God Books 1-4.* Hodder and Stoughton. 1995 – 2017

Whitehouse, Maggy. *The Book of Deborah: The First Book of the Chronicles of Deborah.* Tree of Life Publishing, 2007.

ABOUT THE AUTHOR

Singer / songwriter, Doctor of Philosophy, Reiki Master, Healer, Husband to long-suffering Caroline, Father, Grand Father, ex- 9 to 5 slave and now 60 years young living a life of happiness, peace and health in the West Midlands UK!

Keith Forrest is a first-time author whose personal journey to reveal his true self can only be described as eye-opening, exciting, amazing and inspiring.
From a "normal" job to inner peace and the ability to share, educate and aid those in need, Keith writes from the heart and as his description of his own songs puts it so perfectly; *From the Heart for the Soul.*

Keith is the driving force and Guitarist / Singer / Songwriter for www.theacousticrainbow.co.uk and all the band songs offer the theme, words and message that you can be more, be better, do better and achieve better, but it is up to you to start your own journey.

Keith's own journey started from a dark place, a common trait often displayed by his peers, but his moment of enlightenment and his present-day sense of positivity, healing support and understanding is a true lesson for all.
This book, although a personal journey record, will also serve as a guide for you. If you want to begin your own journey and discover who you really are or can be, Keith's story will without doubt help to influence or motivate you to Health, Peace and Happiness.

The title 'The Spiritual Fruitcake" is a tongue-in -cheek testament to Keith's arrival at his present state of happiness and life with an open mind and smile on his face.

Keith is not a medium and does not describe himself as a spiritualist and often jokes that his only claim to spirituality is that his Aunt was a medium - it said so on the label in her knickers!

Printed in Great Britain
by Amazon